Zero-Knowledge Machine Learning (zkML): Revolutionizing Privacy in AI Applications

Dr Naim Tahir Baig

Published by Dr Naim Tahir Baig, 2025.

ZERO-KNOWLEDGE MACHINE LEARNING (ZKML): REVOLUTIONIZING PRIVACY IN AI APPLICATIONS

First edition. September 8, 2025.

ISBN: 979-8232647858

Written by Dr Naim Tahir Baig.

Also by Dr Naim Tahir Baig

1

Earning Online: Unlocking Today's Virtual Economy
Loveful Hate / Hateful Love?
A Textbook Of Foreign Policy Analysis

Standalone

Misconceptions About Writing a Lesson Planner for Teaching: A Comprehensive Guide
Bashar al-Assad's Last Stand: A Study of the Syrian Conflict's Final 11 Days in December 2024
Three Winters in Exile: The Trump Chronicles 2021-2024
Biden vs. Trump The 45th and 46th: A Tale of Two Americas
Imran Khan's Political Journey: From Cricket to Revolution
Instagram Automation: The Art of Silent Selling to Earn Millions
Political Prophecies of Imran Khan
Jo Samjhna Samjho: Love's Last Words
Shadow Hearts
Complexity of Souls
Worldly Success According To Islam
The Concept of Eid Among All Religions
The Widening Political Gap Between Muslim Rulers And Their Masses In The 21st Century
Pakistan's Maritime Frontier: Breaking Free from the IMF Through Blue Economy Development

Can Russia Help Pakistan Grow?
Why Nuclear-Armed Pakistan Has Not Fought a War Against Israel in the 2020s?
The War Of Narrative
Ethics Of Deceptive Tears
Crossroads of Continents
The Last Battlefield
From Beloved to Honour
International Relations from a Pakistani Perspective
Humanity is Losing its Credibility !
Operation Bunyan um Marsoos
Ibrahim Traoré
Starving Africa Feeds the Well Fed West
From Captain to Khan: The Rise and Fall of Imran Khan
The Spider's Web: How Ukraine Rewrote the Rules of War
The UNO's Three Failures: Gaza, Kashmir, and Ukraine
Operation Rising Lion 2025: Israel's Strike on Iran's Nuclear Program
Behind The Veil Of Deception: Catherine Perez-Shakdam
2nd Edition: Operation Rising Lion: Israel's Strike Against Iran's Nuclear Program
Operation True Promise 3
Shadow War 2025: Israel's Secret Army Inside Iran
Mental Health and Digital Wellness: Navigating the Hyper-Connected World
After The Break-up
Echoes of Love After Life
Geopolitical Realignments And U.S. Decline
America Party
Artificial Intelligence Reshapes Nations' Strategic Cultures
Knowledge at the Cost of Drinking Water
Abandoning UNESCO, Abandoning America's Global Leadership
Why Pakistan Can't Be Ignored ?
Love Seized
Tarifaço: Trump's Tariff Assault on Brazil and the Battle for Hemispheric Power
GAZA: The word 'ETHICS' is at stake

Kiss Cam Crisis

The Boomer Blockade: How an Aging Generation is Reshaping Global Power and Economics at Younger Generations' Expense

Fractured Faith: The Ken Paxton Divorce Scandal and the Crisis of Conservative Authenticity

The New American Empire In 2025

The Last Rock's Secret War: Okinotorishima and Japan's Fight for Tomorrow's Ocean

The Great Realignment

Trump's Siege on the Fed: Politics, Power, and the Fracturing of Global Finance

Nuclear Weapons in Space

Trump vs. Putin: The Secrets Of Alaska Summit 2025

Nuclear Orbits: From Soviet Satellites to Russian Space Power

Learn AI Fast: A Practical Guide for Busy Professionals

Rare Earth Metals in Pakistan: Geopolitics in the New Great Game

The Kulbhushan Affair: Espionage, Diplomacy, and Justice in the Shadow of South Asian Rivalry

Collision Over the Capital: The Untold Story of the 2025 Potomac River Mid-Air Disaster and the Fight for Safer Skies

The Holy Qur'an, Political Fire: The Extremism of Valentina Gomez

World War I of Climate Change: Geopolitical Parallels and Emerging Battles

International Relations: Theoretical Frameworks in the Pakistani Context

Equal and Orderly Multipolarization of the World: The Shanghai Cooperation Organization as a Catalyst

Selbstgehostete E-Mail-Server: Praxisanleitung für Datenschutz und Unabhängigkeit in Deutschland

From Gaza's Siege to Pakistan's Floods 2025: An Islamic Perspective on Collective Accountability and Calamities

Hero's Wings Over the 1965 War: Air Commodore Haider's Story

Zero-Knowledge Machine Learning (zkML): Revolutionizing Privacy in AI Applications

Watch for more at https://www.naimtahirbaig.com.

Table of Contents

To the visionary researchers and practitioners who dared to imagine a world where artificial intelligence serves humanity while preserving human dignity and privacy.

To the open-source communities whose collaborative spirit has made zero-knowledge machine learning accessible to all, democratizing the tools of verifiable AI.

To my family, whose unwavering support and understanding made this exploration of the intersection between cryptography and artificial intelligence possible.

And to the future generations who will inherit the AI systems we build today—may they benefit from technology that is not only intelligent but also fundamentally trustworthy and respectful of human rights.

"In the pursuit of intelligence, we must never abandon wisdom; in the quest for efficiency, we must never sacrifice ethics; and in the development of powerful AI systems, we must always preserve the privacy and agency of those they serve."

"The true measure of artificial intelligence is not merely its capacity to learn and predict, but its ability to do so while preserving the fundamental dignity and privacy of those it serves. Zero-knowledge machine learning represents more than a technological advancement—it embodies our commitment to building AI systems that are accountable without being invasive, verifiable without being transparent to adversaries, and powerful without being dangerous to individual privacy.

In the convergence of cryptography and machine learning, we find not just a solution to technical challenges, but a pathway to ethical AI deployment that honors both human intelligence and human rights. The future belongs to those who can prove their systems work correctly without revealing how they work at all."

— Dr. Naim Tahir Baig

Preface

In an era where artificial intelligence has become ubiquitous in our digital lives—from personalized recommendations that guide our entertainment choices to sophisticated algorithms that assess our creditworthiness—a fundamental tension has emerged between the transformative power of machine learning and the imperative to protect individual privacy. This book addresses one of the most pressing challenges of our time: how to harness the intelligence of AI systems while preserving the confidentiality of sensitive data and maintaining verifiable trust in computational outcomes.

Zero-Knowledge Machine Learning (zkML) represents a paradigm shift that promises to resolve this tension by integrating the cryptographic rigor of zero-knowledge proofs with the computational capabilities of machine learning systems. At its core, zkML enables parties to prove that machine learning computations—whether inference, training, or testing—were performed correctly without revealing the underlying inputs, model parameters, or intermediate computational states. This revolutionary approach opens new possibilities for privacy-preserving AI applications across sectors where data sensitivity and computational integrity are paramount.

The significance of zkML extends far beyond academic curiosity. As recent comprehensive surveys demonstrate, the field has experienced remarkable growth since its inception in 2017, with twenty-seven notable studies published through December 2024 alone. The urgency of this research becomes clear when we consider the current regulatory landscape. The European Union's General Data Protection Regulation (GDPR) has fundamentally transformed how organizations handle personal data, with the European Data Protection Board recently emphasizing that AI development must align with data protection principles of transparency, accountability, and privacy by design. Similar regulatory frameworks are proliferating globally, with the EU AI Act establishing risk-based governance for artificial intelligence systems and numerous U.S. states implementing comprehensive privacy legislation.

The practical implications of these regulatory developments cannot be overstated. Organizations deploying AI systems in healthcare must navigate strict patient confidentiality requirements under regulations like HIPAA, while financial institutions face increasing scrutiny over algorithmic bias and data protection. Traditional approaches often force an uncomfortable choice: either sacrifice privacy by revealing sensitive information or forgo the benefits of AI verification altogether. zkML offers a third path—one that preserves privacy while enabling cryptographic verification of AI computations.

This book is designed for a diverse audience of practitioners and researchers working at the intersection of cryptography, artificial intelligence, and data privacy. AI practitioners and data scientists will find practical guidance on implementing privacy-preserving machine learning systems that comply with emerging regulatory frameworks. Cryptographers and security researchers will discover how established zero-knowledge proof systems can be adapted and optimized for machine learning workloads. Software developers and engineers will gain insights into the tools and frameworks necessary to build zkML applications.

Policymakers and regulatory professionals will benefit from understanding how zkML technologies can address compliance requirements while enabling innovation. Academic researchers will find comprehensive coverage of the theoretical foundations and emerging research directions that define this rapidly evolving field. Graduate students and advanced undergraduates in computer science, mathematics, or related disciplines will discover a structured introduction to both the cryptographic primitives and machine learning concepts essential for understanding zkML.

This book represents the first comprehensive treatment of zero-knowledge machine learning, synthesizing insights from a rapidly expanding body of research. Our methodology draws from peer-reviewed academic papers, technical reports from leading research institutions, and practical implementations from industry pioneers. Given the novelty of the field—no dedicated books on zkML existed prior to this work—we have carefully curated content from the most authoritative sources available.

Our approach prioritizes both theoretical rigor and practical applicability. Each chapter builds systematically on previous concepts, beginning with foundational knowledge of zero-knowledge proofs and machine learning before progressing to advanced implementation techniques and real-world applications. We have included detailed case studies, performance benchmarks, and code examples to bridge the gap between theory and practice.

The content reflects the state of the art as of early 2025, incorporating the latest research findings and technological developments. We have been particularly attentive to the rapid pace of innovation in this field, where performance improvements of several orders of magnitude have been achieved in recent years. Our treatment emphasizes verifiable sources and avoids speculation, focusing instead on documented techniques and empirically validated results.

The book progresses logically from foundational concepts to cutting-edge applications. We begin by establishing the cryptographic underpinnings of zero-knowledge proofs and the machine learning concepts most relevant to zkML implementations. The middle chapters explore practical tools, frameworks, and optimization techniques that enable real-world deployments. The final sections examine current applications across industries and speculate on future research directions.

Throughout this journey, we maintain focus on the transformative potential of zkML to enable trustworthy, privacy-preserving AI systems. The technology promises to unlock new possibilities for collaborative machine learning, verifiable AI governance, and privacy-compliant data utilization. As blockchain networks and decentralized systems increasingly incorporate AI capabilities, zkML provides the cryptographic foundation necessary to maintain trust without sacrificing computational sophistication.

This work would not have been possible without the contributions of numerous researchers, developers, and organizations who have pioneered the zkML field. We extend particular gratitude to the research teams at Worldcoin, whose foundational work on privacy-preserving proof-of-personhood protocols has demonstrated the real-world viability of zkML applications. The innovative contributions of Modulus Labs, including their innovative research on "The Cost of Intelligence" and the development of specialized zkML proving systems, have significantly advanced our understanding of the computational trade-offs inherent in zero-knowledge machine learning.

The development team at Zkonduit deserves special recognition for creating EZKL, a practical library that has democratized access to zkML capabilities and enabled countless researchers and developers to experiment with zero-knowledge proofs for machine learning applications. The broader zkML community, coordinated through initiatives like the awesome-zkml repository and regular community calls, has fostered an environment of open collaboration and knowledge sharing that exemplifies the best traditions of academic and open-source research.

We also acknowledge the Ethereum Foundation and other organizations that have provided crucial funding and institutional support for zkML research. Their investment in this emerging field reflects a recognition that privacy-preserving AI technologies will be essential for the next generation of decentralized applications and trustworthy computing systems.

As we stand at the threshold of an AI-driven future, zkML offers both the tools and the principles necessary to ensure that this future is built on foundations of privacy, verifiability, and trust. We invite readers to join us in exploring this fascinating intersection of cryptography and artificial intelligence, where mathematical elegance meets practical necessity in the service of human dignity and technological progress.

Dr Naim Tahir Baig

The Author

PDS&CE, Pakistan

September 2025

Chapter 1: Foundations of Zero-Knowledge Proofs (ZKPs)

Zero-knowledge proofs represent one of the most elegant and profound achievements in modern cryptography, offering a solution to what once seemed impossible: proving knowledge of a secret without revealing any information about the secret itself. This chapter establishes the fundamental concepts underlying zero-knowledge proof systems, tracing their historical evolution from theoretical constructs to practical cryptographic tools that now power privacy-preserving applications across blockchain networks, machine learning systems, and digital identity platforms.

The emergence of zero-knowledge proofs has fundamentally altered our understanding of what constitutes verifiable computation, enabling new paradigms where privacy and verification need not be mutually exclusive. As we prepare to explore their integration with machine learning in subsequent chapters, understanding these foundational principles becomes essential for appreciating how zkML systems achieve their remarkable capabilities.

1.1 Historical Development of ZKPs

The conceptual foundation of zero-knowledge proofs emerged from decades of research into the fundamental limits of computational proof systems. The journey began in the early 1980s when cryptographers began questioning traditional notions of proof verification and the information disclosure inherent in conventional proof systems.

The Genesis: Interactive Proof Systems

The theoretical groundwork for zero-knowledge proofs was laid in 1985 when three MIT researchers—Shafi Goldwasser, Silvio Micali, and Charles Rackoff—published their seminal paper "The Knowledge Complexity of Interactive Proof Systems."[1] This work introduced the revolutionary concept that proofs could be interactive processes between two parties rather than static mathematical demonstrations.

Goldwasser, Micali, and Rackoff's innovation centered on the recognition that traditional proofs often reveal far more information than necessary to establish the truth of a statement. As they noted in their foundational work, "a proof of a theorem contains more knowledge than the mere fact that the theorem is true."[2] Their insight was that the amount of "knowledge" transmitted in a proof could be precisely quantified and, more importantly, minimized.

The researchers defined zero-knowledge proofs as those that "convey no additional knowledge other than the correctness of the proposition in question."[3] This definition established the theoretical framework for a new class of cryptographic protocols that would prove to have far-reaching implications for privacy-preserving computation.

Expanding the Theoretical Framework

Building upon this foundation, Oded Goldreich, Silvio Micali, and Avi Wigderson made a crucial breakthrough in 1986 by demonstrating that, under certain cryptographic assumptions, zero-knowledge proofs could be constructed for any problem in the complexity class NP.[4] This result was transformative because it showed that zero-knowledge proofs were not limited to specific mathematical problems but could potentially be applied to any computationally verifiable statement.

The theoretical development continued with the introduction of non-interactive zero-knowledge proofs by Manuel Blum, Paul Feldman, and Silvio Micali, who showed that the interaction between prover and verifier could be eliminated through the use of a common random string.[5] This advancement laid the groundwork for the practical implementations that would emerge decades later.

The Emergence of Practical Systems

The transition from theoretical possibility to practical reality began in earnest in the 2010s with the development of efficient zero-knowledge proof systems. The most significant breakthrough came with the introduction of zk-SNARKs (Zero-Knowledge Succinct Non-Interactive Arguments of Knowledge) by Eli Ben-Sasson, Alessandro Chiesa, Eran Tromer, and Madars Virza in their 2013 work "SNARKs for C: Verifying Program Executions Succinctly and in Zero Knowledge."[6]

This work demonstrated that zero-knowledge proofs could be made both succinct (with proof sizes logarithmic in the computation size) and practical for real-world applications. The authors showed how arbitrary program executions could be verified using zk-SNARKs, opening the door to applications in blockchain systems, verifiable computation, and eventually machine learning.

The Quest for Transparency

While zk-SNARKs provided efficiency and succinctness, they relied on trusted setup ceremonies that raised concerns about system transparency and post-quantum security. This limitation motivated the development of zk-STARKs (Zero-Knowledge Scalable Transparent Arguments of Knowledge) by Eli Ben-Sasson, Iddo Bentov, Yinon Horesh, and Michael Riabzev in 2018.[7]

zk-STARKs eliminated the need for trusted setup procedures while maintaining efficiency and adding plausible post-quantum security. As the authors noted, "public trust demands transparency from ZK systems, meaning they be set up with no reliance on any trusted party, and have no trapdoors that could be exploited by powerful parties."[8] This development addressed fundamental concerns about the long-term security and decentralization of zero-knowledge proof systems.

1.2 Core Concepts and Properties

Understanding zero-knowledge proofs requires grasping three fundamental properties that any valid zero-knowledge protocol must satisfy: completeness, soundness, and zero-knowledge. These properties, formalized in the original work by Goldwasser, Micali, and Rackoff, define the security guarantees and functional requirements of zero-knowledge systems.

Completeness: Honest Provers Always Succeed

Completeness ensures that if a statement is true and both the prover and verifier follow the protocol honestly, the verifier will accept the proof with high probability. Formally, for any true statement and honest prover possessing valid witness information, the probability that an honest verifier rejects the proof should be negligible.

This property guarantees that legitimate users will not be falsely rejected by the system. In the context of machine learning applications, completeness ensures that a model owner who genuinely executed a computation correctly will always be able to generate a valid proof of this fact.

Soundness: Dishonest Provers Cannot Fool Verifiers

Soundness, often considered the most critical security property, ensures that no computationally bounded prover can convince an honest verifier to accept a false statement, except with negligible probability. This property protects against malicious actors attempting to claim credit for computations they did not perform or to assert the truth of false statements.

In practice, soundness is often measured by the soundness error—the maximum probability that a dishonest prover can succeed in convincing the verifier of a false statement. Modern zero-knowledge proof systems typically achieve soundness errors of 2^{-120} or better, making successful attacks computationally infeasible.

Zero-Knowledge: Verifiers Learn Nothing Beyond Truth

The zero-knowledge property is perhaps the most conceptually challenging, requiring that the interaction between prover and verifier reveals no information beyond the truth of the statement being proved. Formally, this is captured through the existence of a simulator that can generate transcripts indistinguishable from real protocol executions without knowing the prover's secret information.

The zero-knowledge property is typically formalized through the concept of simulation. If a verifier can learn something from a zero-knowledge proof, then there must exist an efficient algorithm (a simulator) that can produce the same information without interacting with the prover. This requirement ensures that the proof process does not leak any additional knowledge beyond the mere fact that the statement is true.

The Prover-Verifier Model

Zero-knowledge proofs operate within an interactive framework involving two primary parties: the prover and the verifier. The prover possesses secret information (called a witness) that supports the truth of some public statement, while the verifier seeks to confirm the statement's validity without learning the underlying secret.

The interaction typically follows a challenge-response pattern where the prover demonstrates knowledge through responses to random challenges from the verifier. This structure ensures that the prover cannot predict the verifier's challenges in advance, preventing the use of precomputed responses for false statements.

Succinctness and Scalability

Modern zero-knowledge proof systems aim for succinctness, meaning that proof sizes and verification times should be sublinear in the size of the computation being proved. This property is crucial for practical applications, as it enables the verification of large computations using relatively small proofs.

Succinctness is measured along several dimensions: proof size (the amount of data transmitted), prover time (the computational cost of generating a proof), and verifier time (the computational cost of checking a proof). The most advanced systems achieve proof sizes that are polylogarithmic in the computation size and verification times that are independent of the computation complexity.

1.3 Types of ZKP Systems

The landscape of zero-knowledge proof systems has evolved to encompass various approaches, each with distinct characteristics, trade-offs, and optimal use cases. Understanding these different systems is essential for appreciating their applications in machine learning and other domains.

zk-SNARKs: Efficiency Through Preprocessing

Zero-Knowledge Succinct Non-Interactive Arguments of Knowledge represent the most widely deployed class of zero-knowledge proof systems in practical applications. The foundational work by Ben-Sasson et al. established zk-SNARKs as a powerful tool for verifying arbitrary computations with remarkable efficiency.[9]

Structure and Operation: zk-SNARKs operate through a preprocessing phase that generates public parameters specific to the computation being proved. These parameters include a proving key used by the prover to generate proofs and a verification key used by verifiers to check proof validity. The preprocessing phase performs much of the computational heavy lifting, enabling subsequent proof generation and verification to be highly efficient.

Trusted Setup Requirements: The preprocessing phase requires a trusted setup ceremony where random parameters are generated and then securely destroyed. The security of the entire system depends on the assumption that at least one participant in this ceremony honestly deleted their secret parameters. If these "toxic waste" parameters were to be compromised, an attacker could generate false proofs for any statement.

Efficiency Characteristics: zk-SNARKs achieve remarkable efficiency in terms of proof sizes (typically 128-256 bytes) and verification times (a few milliseconds). However, proof generation can be computationally intensive, often requiring several minutes or hours for complex computations. The verification process requires only a constant number of cryptographic operations regardless of the computation size.

Applications and Limitations: zk-SNARKs have found extensive application in blockchain systems, with Zcash being the first major deployment for private cryptocurrency transactions.[10] However, their reliance on trusted setup and vulnerability to quantum attacks have motivated the development of alternative approaches.

zk-STARKs: Transparency and Post-Quantum Security

Zero-Knowledge Scalable Transparent Arguments of Knowledge emerged as a response to the limitations of zk-SNARKs, offering transparency, scalability, and plausible post-quantum security. The work by Ben-Sasson et al. demonstrated that these properties could be achieved without sacrificing practical efficiency.[11]

Transparency and Setup: The most significant advantage of zk-STARKs is their elimination of trusted setup requirements. Instead of relying on secret parameters, zk-STARKs use publicly verifiable randomness, making the system "transparent" in the sense that no hidden trapdoors can compromise security. This transparency addresses fundamental concerns about long-term security and centralization.

Scalability Properties: zk-STARKs achieve true scalability with proof generation times that scale quasi-linearly with computation size and verification times that scale polylogarithmically. For large computations, this scaling often makes zk-STARKs more efficient than zk-SNARKs despite larger constant factors.

Quantum Resistance: Unlike zk-SNARKs, which rely on elliptic curve cryptography vulnerable to quantum attacks, zk-STARKs are based on hash functions and error-correcting codes that are believed to resist quantum cryptanalysis. This property makes zk-STARKs attractive for long-term security applications.

Trade-offs: The main disadvantage of zk-STARKs is significantly larger proof sizes, typically ranging from tens of kilobytes to several megabytes depending on the computation complexity. This makes them less suitable for bandwidth-constrained applications but acceptable for many blockchain and machine learning use cases.

Bulletproofs: Range Proofs and Beyond

Bulletproofs, introduced by Benedikt Bünz and colleagues in 2017, represent a specialized class of zero-knowledge proofs optimized for specific types of statements, particularly range proofs.[12] While not as general as zk-SNARKs or zk-STARKs, Bulletproofs offer unique advantages for certain applications.

Specialized Efficiency: Bulletproofs achieve logarithmic proof sizes for range proofs and other specialized statements without requiring trusted setup. For applications like proving that a committed value lies within a specific range, Bulletproofs offer superior efficiency compared to general-purpose systems.

Limited Scope: Unlike zk-SNARKs and zk-STARKs, which can handle arbitrary computations, Bulletproofs are optimized for specific types of mathematical relationships. This specialization limits their applicability but enables exceptional efficiency within their domain.

PLONK: Universal Setup and Flexibility

PLONK (Permutations over Lagrange-bases for Oecumenical Noninteractive arguments of Knowledge) represents a significant advancement in zero-knowledge proof systems by introducing the concept of universal setup.[13] Unlike zk-SNARKs, which require circuit-specific trusted setup, PLONK uses a single universal setup that can be reused across different computations.

Universal Setup: PLONK's universal setup generates public parameters that can be used to prove any computation up to a maximum size bound. This eliminates the need for repeated trusted setup ceremonies when deploying new applications, significantly reducing operational complexity and security concerns.

Customizable Gates: PLONK supports custom gates that can efficiently encode domain-specific operations. This flexibility has made PLONK particularly attractive for zero-knowledge machine learning applications, where specialized operations like activation functions can be implemented as custom gates.

1.4 Mathematical Foundations

The practical implementation of zero-knowledge proofs relies on sophisticated mathematical constructions that transform computational problems into forms amenable to cryptographic proof systems. Understanding these foundations is crucial for appreciating how complex computations, including machine learning algorithms, can be verified using zero-knowledge techniques.

Arithmetic Circuits: The Computational Model

Arithmetic circuits provide the fundamental computational model underlying most zero-knowledge proof systems. Unlike boolean circuits that operate on binary values, arithmetic circuits perform operations over finite fields, enabling efficient encoding of mathematical computations.

Structure and Operations: An arithmetic circuit consists of gates that perform addition and multiplication operations over a finite field. Each gate takes one or more inputs and produces a single output, with the constraint that all operations must be linear combinations (for addition gates) or products (for multiplication gates) of the inputs. This restriction ensures that the circuit can be efficiently converted into constraint systems suitable for zero-knowledge proofs.

Gate Types and Constraints: The most common gates in arithmetic circuits are addition gates, multiplication gates, and constant multiplication gates. Addition gates are "free" in most zero-knowledge systems because linear operations can be performed efficiently. Multiplication gates, however, represent the primary computational bottleneck and typically determine the complexity of the resulting proof system.

Finite Field Arithmetic: All operations within arithmetic circuits are performed modulo a large prime number, creating a finite field. This mathematical structure ensures that all operations are well-defined and that intermediate values do not grow unboundedly. The choice of field size represents a trade-off between security (larger fields are more secure) and efficiency (smaller fields enable faster computation).

Rank-1 Constraint Systems (R1CS)

Rank-1 Constraint Systems provide a standardized intermediate representation for arithmetic circuits that can be efficiently processed by zero-knowledge proof systems. R1CS transforms the circuit representation into a system of quadratic equations that capture the computational relationships.

Mathematical Definition: An R1CS consists of three matrices (A, B, C) and a witness vector w such that $(Aw) \circ (Bw) = Cw$, where $\circ$ denotes element-wise multiplication (Hadamard product). Each row of these matrices represents a constraint corresponding to a multiplication gate in the original arithmetic circuit.[14]

Constraint Generation: The process of converting an arithmetic circuit to R1CS involves creating one constraint for each multiplication gate. For a gate computing $z = x \times y$, the corresponding constraint ensures that the relationship holds for the witness values. Addition gates and linear combinations are handled implicitly through the matrix structure.

Witness Structure: The witness vector w contains all intermediate values computed during the circuit execution, including inputs, outputs, and intermediate results. The first element of the witness is typically set to 1 to handle constant terms. A valid witness satisfies all R1CS constraints, corresponding to a correct execution of the original computation.

Optimization Techniques: Modern R1CS generation involves numerous optimization techniques to minimize the number of constraints. These include common subexpression elimination, gate merging, and specialized constraint patterns for common operations. Reducing constraint count directly translates to improved efficiency in the resulting zero-knowledge proof.

Polynomial Commitments: Enabling Succinct Proofs

Polynomial commitments form the cryptographic foundation that enables succinct zero-knowledge proofs. These schemes allow a prover to commit to a polynomial and later prove evaluations of that polynomial without revealing the polynomial itself.

The KZG Commitment Scheme: The most widely used polynomial commitment scheme was introduced by Aniket Kate, Gregory Zaverucha, and Ian Goldberg in 2010.[15] The KZG scheme enables constant-size commitments to polynomials of arbitrary degree and constant-size proofs of polynomial evaluations.

Trusted Setup and Structure: KZG commitments require a trusted setup phase that generates a structured reference string (SRS) consisting of powers of a secret value τ multiplied by a generator point: $[g, \tau g, \tau^2 g, ..., \tau^d g]$. The secret value τ must be deleted after setup to maintain security. The commitment to a polynomial $f(x) = \Sigma_i a_i x_i$ is computed as $\Sigma_i a_i(\tau_i g)$.

Evaluation Proofs: To prove that f(a) = y for some point a and value y, the prover computes a quotient polynomial q(x) = (f(x) - y)/(x - a) and provides the commitment g^(q(τ)) as the proof. The verifier can check this proof using a bilinear pairing operation that verifies the polynomial remainder theorem at the secret point τ.

Batch Proofs and Aggregation: KZG commitments support efficient batch proofs that can simultaneously prove multiple evaluations of the same polynomial or evaluations of different polynomials at the same point. This capability is crucial for achieving efficiency in complex zero-knowledge proof systems.

The Fiat-Shamir Heuristic: Achieving Non-Interactivity

The Fiat-Shamir heuristic provides a general technique for converting interactive zero-knowledge proofs into non-interactive ones, eliminating the need for real-time communication between prover and verifier. This transformation is essential for practical applications where interaction is impractical or impossible.

Transformation Mechanism: The Fiat-Shamir heuristic replaces the verifier's random challenges with outputs from a cryptographic hash function applied to the proof transcript up to that point. Instead of the verifier sending a random challenge c, the prover computes c = H(transcript), where H is a cryptographic hash function and transcript contains all previous messages.[16]

Security in the Random Oracle Model: The security of the Fiat-Shamir transformation is typically analyzed in the random oracle model, where the hash function is assumed to behave like a truly random function. Under this assumption, the non-interactive proof maintains the same security properties as the original interactive proof. However, instantiating the random oracle with a concrete hash function requires careful analysis.

Practical Considerations: When applying the Fiat-Shamir heuristic, several practical considerations arise. The hash function must be collision-resistant and should produce outputs that are indistinguishable from random. The transcript must include all relevant public information to prevent attacks where the prover manipulates the challenge generation process.

Application in Modern Systems: The Fiat-Shamir heuristic is ubiquitous in modern zero-knowledge proof systems, enabling their deployment in blockchain applications, verifiable computation systems, and machine learning verification. Most practical zk-SNARK and zk-STARK implementations rely on this technique to achieve non-interactivity.

The foundations established in this chapter provide the essential background for understanding how zero-knowledge proofs can be applied to machine learning systems. The mathematical constructions of arithmetic circuits, R1CS, polynomial commitments, and the Fiat-Shamir heuristic will reappear throughout our exploration of zkML, where they enable the verification of complex machine learning computations while preserving privacy and enabling scalability.

As we transition to examining machine learning fundamentals in the next chapter, these cryptographic primitives will serve as the building blocks for creating privacy-preserving AI systems that can prove their computations without revealing sensitive model parameters, training data, or intermediate results. The marriage of these cryptographic techniques with machine learning represents one of the most promising developments in privacy-enhancing technologies.

Footnotes:

[1] Shafi Goldwasser, Silvio Micali, and Charles Rackoff, "The Knowledge Complexity of Interactive Proof Systems," SIAM Journal on Computing 18, no. 1 (1989): 186-208.

[2] Ibid., 186.

[3] Ibid., 187.

[4] Oded Goldreich, Silvio Micali, and Avi Wigderson, "Proofs that Yield Nothing But Their Validity or All Languages in NP Have Zero-Knowledge Proof Systems," Journal of the ACM 38, no. 3 (1991): 690-728.

[5] Manuel Blum, Paul Feldman, and Silvio Micali, "Non-Interactive Zero-Knowledge and Its Applications," in Proceedings of the Twentieth Annual ACM Symposium on Theory of Computing (New York: ACM, 1988), 103-112.

[6] Eli Ben-Sasson et al., "SNARKs for C: Verifying Program Executions Succinctly and in Zero Knowledge," in Advances in Cryptology – CRYPTO 2013, ed. Ran Canetti and Juan A. Garay (Berlin: Springer, 2013), 90-108.

[7] Eli Ben-Sasson et al., "Scalable, Transparent, and Post-quantum Secure Computational Integrity," Cryptology ePrint Archive, Report 2018/046 (2018), https://eprint.iacr.org/2018/046.

[8] Ibid., 1.

[9] Ben-Sasson et al., "SNARKs for C," 90-108.

[10] Eli Ben-Sasson et al., "Zerocash: Decentralized Anonymous Payments from Bitcoin," in 2014 IEEE Symposium on Security and Privacy (Los Alamitos: IEEE Computer Society, 2014), 459-474.

[11] Ben-Sasson et al., "Scalable, Transparent, and Post-quantum Secure Computational Integrity."

[12] Benedikt Bünz et al., "Bulletproofs: Short Proofs for Confidential Transactions and More," in 2018 IEEE Symposium on Security and Privacy (Los Alamitos: IEEE Computer Society, 2018), 315-334.

[13] Ariel Gabizon, Zachary J. Williamson, and Oana Ciobotaru, "PLONK: Permutations over Lagrange-bases for Oecumenical Noninteractive arguments of Knowledge," Cryptology ePrint Archive, Report 2019/953 (2019), https://eprint.iacr.org/2019/953.

[14] Bhaskar Krishnamachari, "Understanding Zero-Knowledge Proofs: Part 5-Arithmetic Circuits and R1CS," Medium, July 14, 2024, https://medium.com/@bhaskark2/understanding-zero-knowledge-proofs-part-5-arithmetic-circuits-and-r1cs-be66347096b8.

[15] Aniket Kate, Gregory M. Zaverucha, and Ian Goldberg, "Constant-Size Commitments to Polynomials and Their Applications," in Advances in Cryptology – ASIACRYPT 2010, ed. Masayuki Abe (Berlin: Springer, 2010), 177-194.

[16] Amos Fiat and Adi Shamir, "How to Prove Yourself: Practical Solutions to Identification and Signature Problems," in Advances in Cryptology – CRYPTO '86, ed. Andrew M. Odlyzko (Berlin: Springer, 1987), 186-194.

Chapter 2: Fundamentals of Machine Learning

As artificial intelligence transforms industries from healthcare to finance, machine learning serves as the foundational technology enabling computers to learn patterns from data and make intelligent decisions.[1] This chapter establishes the essential concepts underlying machine learning that are necessary for understanding zero-knowledge machine learning (zkML) systems. While deep learning has demonstrated remarkable capabilities across diverse domains from protein folding in biology to molecular discovery in chemistry and particle interactions in physics,[2] the integration of zero-knowledge proofs with machine learning requires a thorough understanding of how these systems process data, learn patterns, and generate predictions.

The relevance of machine learning fundamentals to zkML cannot be overstated. As we will explore in subsequent chapters, zkML systems must prove that machine learning computations were performed correctly without revealing sensitive inputs, model parameters, or outputs. This requires translating traditional ML operations into cryptographic circuits, making it essential to understand the mathematical foundations and computational processes that underlie modern machine learning systems.

2.1 Overview of Machine Learning Paradigms

Machine learning encompasses several distinct paradigms, each addressing different types of learning problems and data scenarios. Understanding these paradigms is crucial for zkML applications, as different learning approaches present unique challenges and opportunities for zero-knowledge proof integration.

Supervised Learning

Supervised learning represents the most fundamental machine learning paradigm, where algorithms learn from labeled training data to make predictions on new, unseen data.[3] In supervised learning, the training dataset consists of input-output pairs (x, y), where x represents the input features and y represents the known target or label. The goal is to learn a function f that maps inputs to outputs such that $f(x) \approx y$.

Classification Tasks: In classification, the target variable y represents discrete categories or classes. For example, in image classification—a domain where convolutional neural networks have achieved remarkable success[4]—the task might involve categorizing images into classes such as "cat," "dog," or "car." The ImageNet challenge, where AlexNet demonstrated the potential of deep convolutional neural networks in 2012, marked a significant milestone in image recognition tasks.[5] Classification algorithms learn decision boundaries that separate different classes in the feature space.

Regression Tasks: Regression problems involve predicting continuous numerical values. For instance, predicting house prices based on features like location, size, and amenities represents a typical regression problem. Linear regression, one of the simplest supervised learning algorithms, attempts to find the best-fitting line through the data points by minimizing the squared differences between predicted and actual values.

Key Components of Supervised Learning:

1. **Data Preprocessing**: Raw data must be cleaned, normalized, and transformed into suitable formats. This includes handling missing values, scaling features to similar ranges, and encoding categorical variables.
2. **Training Process**: The algorithm iteratively adjusts its parameters to minimize prediction errors on the training data. This typically involves defining a loss function that measures the difference between predicted and actual outputs.
3. **Validation and Testing**: The trained model is evaluated on separate validation and test sets to assess its generalization capability and avoid overfitting.

Unsupervised Learning

Unsupervised learning addresses scenarios where only input data is available without corresponding labels.[6] This paradigm focuses on discovering hidden patterns, structures, or relationships within the data. Unsupervised learning is particularly valuable in exploratory data analysis and feature extraction.

Clustering: Clustering algorithms group similar data points together based on their inherent characteristics. K-means clustering, for example, partitions data into k clusters by minimizing within-cluster variance. Hierarchical clustering creates tree-like structures showing relationships between data points at different levels of granularity.

Dimensionality Reduction: These techniques reduce the number of features while preserving important information. Principal Component Analysis (PCA) identifies the directions of maximum variance in the data and projects it onto lower-dimensional subspaces. This is particularly useful for visualization and computational efficiency.

Association Rule Learning: This discovers relationships between different variables, such as "customers who buy bread also tend to buy butter," commonly used in market basket analysis.

Reinforcement Learning

Reinforcement learning (RL) represents a paradigm where agents learn to make decisions through interaction with an environment, receiving rewards or penalties based on their actions.[7] Unlike supervised learning, RL does not rely on labeled examples but instead learns through trial and error.

Key RL Components:

- **Agent**: The decision-making entity
- **Environment**: The external system the agent interacts with
- **State**: Current situation of the agent
- **Action**: Choices available to the agent
- **Reward**: Feedback signal indicating the quality of actions

The agent's goal is to learn a policy—a mapping from states to actions—that maximizes cumulative reward over time. Despite its prominence in research, reinforcement learning constitutes a small fraction of real-world AI applications, with estimates suggesting less than 5% of deployed AI systems rely on RL in 2025.[8]

Applications in zkML Context: While RL applications in zkML are limited due to computational complexity, the paradigm's emphasis on sequential decision-making and reward optimization presents interesting possibilities for privacy-preserving multi-agent systems and decentralized learning scenarios.

2.2 Neural Networks and Deep Learning

Neural networks form the computational backbone of modern machine learning, providing the foundation for deep learning systems that have revolutionized artificial intelligence.[9] Understanding neural network architectures and their training mechanisms is essential for zkML, as these systems must be translated into zero-knowledge proof circuits.

Basic Neural Network Architecture

An artificial neural network consists of interconnected nodes (neurons) organized in layers. Each neuron receives inputs, applies a transformation, and produces an output. The basic mathematical operation of a neuron can be expressed as:

$$output = f(\Sigma(wi \times xi) + b)$$

where wi represents weights, xi represents inputs, b is the bias term, and f is the activation function.[10]

Layer Types:

1. **Input Layer**: Receives raw data and passes it to subsequent layers
2. **Hidden Layers**: Perform computations and feature extraction
3. **Output Layer**: Produces final predictions or classifications

Activation Functions

Activation functions introduce non-linearity into neural networks, enabling them to learn complex patterns beyond simple linear relationships.[11] The choice of activation function significantly impacts network performance and training dynamics.

Sigmoid Function: The sigmoid function maps input values to the range (0, 1), making it useful for binary classification problems. Mathematically defined as $\sigma(x) = 1/(1 + e^\wedge(-x))$, the sigmoid function has smooth gradients but suffers from vanishing gradient problems in deep networks.[12]

Rectified Linear Unit (ReLU): ReLU has become the most popular activation function in deep learning due to its computational simplicity and effectiveness in mitigating vanishing gradient problems. Defined as $f(x) = \max(0, x)$, ReLU outputs the input directly if positive, otherwise zero.[13] This simplicity makes ReLU particularly attractive for zkML implementations, as it reduces the complexity of cryptographic circuit representations.

Hyperbolic Tangent (tanh): Similar to sigmoid but mapping inputs to the range (-1, 1), tanh often provides better performance for hidden layers by centering data around zero.

Backpropagation Algorithm

Backpropagation represents the fundamental training algorithm for neural networks, using the chain rule of calculus to compute gradients and update network parameters.[14] The algorithm consists of two main phases:

Forward Pass: Data flows through the network from input to output layers, with each neuron computing its activation based on inputs from the previous layer. During this phase, the network generates predictions that are compared to actual targets.

Backward Pass: Error signals propagate backward through the network, computing gradients for each parameter. The gradient of the loss function with respect to each weight indicates how much that weight should be adjusted to reduce prediction error.

The mathematical foundation of backpropagation relies on the chain rule:

$$\partial L/\partial w = \partial L/\partial y \times \partial y/\partial z \times \partial z/\partial w$$

where L represents the loss function, y is the output, z is the pre-activation, and w is the weight.[15]

Challenges in Deep Networks: As networks become deeper, gradients can become very small (vanishing gradients) or very large (exploding gradients), making training difficult. The vanishing gradient problem is particularly pronounced with sigmoid and tanh activation functions, where gradients can approach zero in deeper layers.[16]

Convolutional Neural Networks

Convolutional Neural Networks (CNNs) represent specialized architectures designed for processing grid-like data such as images.[17] CNNs use convolution operations to detect local patterns and hierarchical features.

Convolutional Layers: These layers apply filters (kernels) across input data to detect features like edges, textures, and patterns. Each filter produces a feature map highlighting specific patterns in the input.

Pooling Layers: Pooling operations downsample feature maps to reduce computational complexity and provide translation invariance. Max pooling, for example, selects the maximum value in each patch of the feature map.

CNN Success in Image Classification: The success of CNNs in image classification, demonstrated by architectures like LeNet, AlexNet, and ResNet, has established them as the dominant approach for computer vision tasks.[18] ResNet's introduction of skip connections allowed training of very deep networks by enabling gradients to flow more effectively through the network.

Recurrent Neural Networks

Recurrent Neural Networks (RNNs) handle sequential data by maintaining hidden states that capture information from previous time steps.[19] This capability makes RNNs suitable for tasks involving time series, natural language processing, and any scenario where temporal dependencies matter.

LSTM Networks: Long Short-Term Memory networks address the vanishing gradient problem in standard RNNs by introducing memory cells with gating mechanisms.[20] The three gates—input, forget, and output—control information flow and enable learning of long-range dependencies.

Bidirectional RNNs: These networks process sequences in both forward and backward directions, providing comprehensive context for each time step. This approach is particularly effective for tasks where the entire sequence is available, such as machine translation or sentiment analysis.

Deep Learning Revolution

Deep learning, utilizing neural networks with multiple hidden layers, has transformed artificial intelligence by enabling automatic feature learning from raw data.[21] The depth of these networks allows them to learn increasingly abstract representations, with lower layers detecting simple features and higher layers combining them into complex concepts.

Universal Approximation Theorem: This theorem states that a neural network with a single hidden layer containing sufficient neurons can approximate any continuous function to arbitrary accuracy.[22] This theoretical foundation explains why neural networks can model complex relationships in data.

2.3 Privacy Challenges in Traditional ML

The integration of machine learning into sensitive domains has revealed significant privacy challenges that zkML aims to address. Understanding these challenges provides crucial context for appreciating the value proposition of zero-knowledge machine learning systems.

Data Leakage in Federated Learning

Federated learning was designed to enable collaborative model training while keeping data decentralized, ostensibly preserving privacy.[23] However, research has revealed that federated learning systems are vulnerable to various privacy attacks that can expose sensitive information about participants' data.

Gradient Inversion Attacks: Even though raw data never leaves local devices in federated learning, the model updates (gradients) shared with central servers can leak significant information about training data. Gradient inversion techniques can reconstruct training samples from gradient information with surprising fidelity.[24] These attacks exploit the fact that gradients carry information about the data used to compute them.

Membership Inference Attacks: Adversaries can determine whether specific data points were used in training by analyzing model behavior. This type of attack poses particular risks in healthcare and financial domains where membership information itself is sensitive.[25]

Model Inversion Attacks: These attacks attempt to reconstruct input data from model outputs or parameters. In image classification scenarios, attackers might reconstruct facial features from a model trained to recognize faces, even without access to the original training data.[26]

Regulatory Compliance Challenges

Modern privacy regulations impose strict requirements on data handling and processing, creating significant challenges for traditional machine learning approaches.

General Data Protection Regulation (GDPR): The European Union's GDPR mandates explicit consent for data processing, the right to data portability, and the right to be forgotten.[27] Traditional machine learning models struggle to comply with these requirements, particularly the right to deletion, as removing specific training examples from trained models is technically challenging.

Health Insurance Portability and Accountability Act (HIPAA): In healthcare applications, HIPAA requires strict protection of protected health information (PHI).[28] Machine learning models trained on health data must ensure that individual patient information cannot be inferred from model behavior or outputs.

Data Minimization Principle: GDPR's data minimization principle requires that only data necessary for the specified purpose be collected and processed.[29] Federated learning partially addresses this by avoiding centralized data collection, but the gradient sharing mechanism still presents privacy risks.

Information Leakage Through Model Outputs

Traditional machine learning models can inadvertently leak information about their training data through various channels:

Statistical Inference: Attackers can perform statistical analysis on model outputs to infer properties of the training data distribution. This is particularly concerning when training data contains sensitive demographic or health information.

Model Extraction: Adversaries can query machine learning models to extract information about their architecture, parameters, or training data. This is especially problematic for Machine Learning as a Service (MLaaS) platforms where models are exposed through APIs.[30]

Side-Channel Attacks: Information can leak through timing analysis, power consumption patterns, or other side channels during model inference, particularly in edge computing scenarios.

Privacy Challenges in Distributed Learning

Beyond federated learning, other distributed learning paradigms face similar privacy challenges:

Split Learning: In split learning, models are divided between client and server, with intermediate representations shared during training. However, these intermediate features can still leak information about input data.[31]

Collaborative Learning: When multiple organizations collaborate to train models, ensuring that no participant learns about others' data while still benefiting from the collaboration remains challenging.

Trust and Verification Issues

Traditional machine learning systems often operate as "black boxes," making it difficult to verify that they behave correctly without access to training data or model internals.[32]

Model Integrity: Ensuring that models have not been tampered with or poisoned during training or deployment is crucial for sensitive applications. Traditional systems lack mechanisms to prove computational integrity.

Data Provenance: Verifying the source and quality of training data without exposing the data itself presents significant challenges in collaborative learning scenarios.

2.4 Verifiability in ML

The need for verifiable machine learning has emerged as a critical requirement in high-stakes applications where model decisions have significant consequences. This section explores the challenges of black-box models and introduces the concept of verifiable inference as a bridge to zero-knowledge machine learning.

The Black-Box Problem

Modern machine learning models, particularly deep learning systems, operate as "black boxes" where the decision-making process is opaque to users and stakeholders.[33] This opacity creates several challenges:

Lack of Transparency: Complex models with millions or billions of parameters make decisions through intricate computational processes that are difficult to interpret or explain. This lack of transparency is particularly problematic in domains like healthcare, criminal justice, and financial services where algorithmic decisions significantly impact human lives.[34]

Trust and Accountability: The inability to understand how models reach their conclusions undermines trust and makes it difficult to hold systems accountable for their decisions. Recent research has shown that these concerns are well-founded, as machine learning models can exhibit unexpected behaviors and biases.[35]

Regulatory Compliance: Many jurisdictions now require algorithmic transparency and explainability, particularly in automated decision-making systems. The European Union's proposed AI Act and similar regulations worldwide emphasize the need for interpretable AI systems in high-risk applications.

Computational Integrity in Machine Learning

Computational integrity refers to the ability to verify that a computation was performed correctly without re-executing the entire process.[36] In the context of machine learning, this means proving that model inference or training was conducted according to specified algorithms and parameters.

Verification Challenges: Traditional machine learning systems provide no cryptographic guarantees about the correctness of their computations. Users must trust that:

- The model architecture matches what was claimed
- The training process followed specified protocols
- Inference computations are performed correctly
- No malicious modifications were made to the model

Need for Cryptographic Guarantees: As machine learning models are deployed in increasingly critical applications, the need for cryptographic proof of computational correctness becomes paramount. This is particularly important in:

- Medical diagnosis systems where incorrect computations could lead to misdiagnosis
- Financial trading algorithms where computational errors could result in significant losses

- Autonomous vehicle systems where safety depends on correct model behavior

Verifiable Inference as a Bridge to zkML

Verifiable inference represents an intermediate step between traditional machine learning and full zero-knowledge machine learning systems. The goal is to prove that model inference was performed correctly while potentially revealing some information about inputs or outputs.

Proof Systems for ML: Several cryptographic proof systems can be adapted for machine learning verification:

- **SNARKs (Succinct Non-Interactive Arguments of Knowledge)**: These provide short proofs that can be verified efficiently
- **STARKs (Scalable Transparent Arguments of Knowledge)**: These offer transparency without trusted setup requirements
- **Interactive proof systems**: These allow for verification through multiple rounds of interaction between prover and verifier

Circuit Representation: To enable cryptographic verification, machine learning computations must be expressed as arithmetic circuits over finite fields. This transformation presents several challenges:

- **Non-linear operations**: Activation functions like ReLU and sigmoid must be approximated or implemented using circuit-friendly operations
- **Floating-point arithmetic**: Most ML frameworks use floating-point operations, which must be converted to fixed-point or integer arithmetic for circuit implementations
- **Scaling complexity**: The size of circuits grows significantly with model complexity, making verification of large models computationally challenging[37]

Applications of Verifiable ML

Several domains have begun exploring verifiable machine learning to address trust and integrity concerns:

Healthcare AI: Medical AI systems require verification that diagnostic models perform correctly, especially when processing sensitive patient data. Verifiable inference can provide cryptographic guarantees about diagnostic accuracy without revealing patient information.[38]

Financial Services: Algorithmic trading and credit scoring systems need verification to ensure fair and correct decision-making. Verifiable ML can prove that models operate according to regulatory requirements without exposing proprietary algorithms.

Decentralized Systems: Blockchain and decentralized applications require verifiable off-chain computations. ML models running off-chain can use verification proofs to convince on-chain systems of their correct execution.

Limitations and Challenges

Current approaches to verifiable machine learning face several limitations:

Computational Overhead: Generating proofs for ML computations can be orders of magnitude slower than direct execution, limiting practical applicability for real-time systems.

Circuit Complexity: Large neural networks require enormous circuits, making proof generation and verification computationally intensive. Current systems are limited to relatively small models compared to state-of-the-art deep learning systems.

Accuracy Trade-offs: Circuit representations may require approximations of certain operations, potentially affecting model accuracy. The trade-off between verifiability and performance remains an active area of research.

Future Directions

The evolution toward zero-knowledge machine learning represents the natural progression of verifiable ML systems. By combining computational integrity with privacy preservation, zkML systems promise to enable:

Privacy-Preserving Verification: Proving correct computation without revealing sensitive inputs, model parameters, or outputs

Scalable Proof Systems: Development of more efficient proof systems that can handle large-scale machine learning models

Standardization: Establishment of standards and frameworks for verifiable ML across different domains and applications

The foundation laid by verifiable inference systems provides the necessary groundwork for understanding how zero-knowledge proofs can be integrated with machine learning computations, setting the stage for the zkML revolution explored in subsequent chapters.

Footnotes:

[1] Al-Jumaili, Ahmed H. A., et al. "Big Data Analytics Using Cloud Computing Based Frameworks for Power Management Systems: Status, Constraints, and Future Recommendations." Sensors 23, no. 6 (2023): 2952.

[2] O'Halloran, T., et al. "A Comprehensive Review of Deep Learning: Architectures, Recent Advances, and Applications." Information 15, no. 12 (2024): 755.

[3] Peng, Y., et al. "Machine Learning: Algorithms, Real-World Applications and Research Directions." SN Computer Science 2, no. 3 (2021): 160.

[4] Krizhevsky, Alex, Ilya Sutskever, and Geoffrey E. Hinton. "ImageNet Classification with Deep Convolutional Neural Networks." Communications of the ACM 60, no. 6 (2017): 84-90.

[5] Ibid.

[6] "Machine Learning: Algorithms, Real-World Applications and Research Directions," SN Computer Science.

[7] James Fahey, "The State of Reinforcement Learning in 2025: Foundations, Frontiers, and Future Applications," Medium, July 17, 2025.

[8] Ibid.

[9] "A Comprehensive Review of Deep Learning: Architectures, Recent Advances, and Applications," Information.

[10] "A Thorough Review on Deep Learning Neural Network," IEEE Conference Publication, 2023.

[11] "Activation Functions in Neural Networks," GeeksforGeeks, June 3, 2025.

[12] "A Comprehensive Review of Deep Learning: Architectures, Recent Advances, and Applications," Information.

[13] Ibid.

[14] "Backpropagation in Neural Network," GeeksforGeeks, July 1, 2025.

[15] "A Step by Step Backpropagation Example," Matt Mazur, February 23, 2024.

[16] "Neural Networks: Forward Pass and Backpropagation," Towards Data Science, March 5, 2025.

[17] "A Comprehensive Review of Deep Learning: Architectures, Recent Advances, and Applications," Information.

[18] Ibid.

[19] Ibid.

[20] Ibid.

[21] Ibid.

[22] Ibid.

[23] "Federated Learning Privacy: Attacks, Defenses, Applications, and Policy Landscape — A Survey," arXiv preprint arXiv:2405.03636, May 15, 2024.

[24] Ibid.

[25] "A Survey of Privacy Attacks in Machine Learning," ACM Computing Surveys 56, no. 4 (2024): 1-37.

[26] "GitHub - stratosphereips/awesome-ml-privacy-attacks: An awesome list of papers on privacy attacks against machine learning," accessed September 8, 2025.

[27] "Privacy preservation in federated learning: An insightful survey from the GDPR perspective," Computers & Security 106 (2021): 102261.

[28] "Privacy preservation for federated learning in health care," PMC, 2024.

[29] "Privacy preservation in federated learning: An insightful survey from the GDPR perspective," Computers & Security.

[30] "A Survey of Privacy Attacks in Machine Learning," ACM Computing Surveys.

[31] "Threats, attacks and defenses to federated learning: issues, taxonomy and perspectives," Cybersecurity 5, no. 1 (2022): 1-19.

[32] "Interpreting Black-Box Models: A Review on Explainable Artificial Intelligence," Cognitive Computation 15, no. 5 (2023): 1688-1703.

[33] Ibid.

[34] "Stop Explaining Black Box Machine Learning Models for High Stakes Decisions and Use Interpretable Models Instead," arXiv preprint arXiv:1811.10154, September 22, 2019.

[35] "Explainability, transparency and black box challenges of AI in radiology: impact on patient care in cardiovascular radiology," Egyptian Journal of Radiology and Nuclear Medicine 55, no. 183 (2024).

[36] "Towards Stricter Black-box Integrity Verification of Deep Neural Network Models," Proceedings of the 32nd ACM International Conference on Multimedia, 2024.

[37] "Verifiable evaluations of machine learning models using zero-knowledge proofs," arXiv preprint arXiv:2402.02675, 2024.

[38] "Demystifying the black box: A survey on explainable artificial intelligence (XAI) in bioinformatics," Computational and Structural Biotechnology Journal 27 (2025): 346-359.

Chapter 3: The Emergence of zkML

The convergence of zero-knowledge proofs and machine learning represents one of the most significant developments in both cryptography and artificial intelligence since 2020. This integration, termed zero-knowledge machine learning (zkML), has emerged as a revolutionary approach to addressing fundamental challenges in modern AI deployment: the need for verifiable computation, privacy preservation, and trustless execution. As machine learning models increasingly power critical decisions across industries—from financial trading algorithms to medical diagnostics—the ability to prove their correct execution without revealing sensitive data has become paramount.

The emergence of zkML represents more than a technical innovation; it embodies a paradigm shift toward verifiable, privacy-preserving AI systems that can operate in adversarial environments. This chapter explores how zkML has evolved from theoretical possibility to practical implementation, examining its core principles, workflows, and the revolutionary innovations that make it possible to prove machine learning computations with mathematical certainty.

3.1 Defining zkML

Zero-knowledge machine learning (zkML) fundamentally represents the application of zero-knowledge proof systems to machine learning computations, enabling parties to prove that specific ML operations—particularly inference—were performed correctly without revealing the underlying model parameters, input data, or intermediate computations.[1] At its core, zkML addresses a critical trust problem in contemporary AI deployment: how can one verify that a claimed machine learning result actually originated from a specific model and input, particularly when the model provider has legitimate reasons to keep their intellectual property confidential?

The formal definition of zkML extends the traditional zero-knowledge proof framework to encompass machine learning operations. In a zkML system, a prover can demonstrate to a verifier that they correctly executed an ML model

M on input data *x* to produce output *y*, such that $y = M(x)$, without revealing any information about the model weights, the input data, or intermediate activations beyond what can be inferred from the final output itself.[2] This capability is achieved by converting the ML model into an arithmetic circuit representation that can be proven using zero-knowledge proof systems such as zk-SNARKs or zk-STARKs.

Distinguishing zkML from Related Technologies

It is crucial to distinguish zkML from other privacy-preserving machine learning approaches, particularly fully homomorphic encryption (FHE). While FHE enables computations on encrypted data, producing encrypted results that reveal nothing about the underlying data when decrypted,[3] zkML provides a different guarantee: it proves that computations were performed correctly but does not necessarily hide all aspects of the computation. The key distinction lies in their objectives—FHE prioritizes data privacy during computation, while zkML prioritizes computational integrity and selective privacy.

The relationship between zkML and traditional secure multi-party computation (SMPC) also merits clarification. SMPC enables multiple parties to jointly compute a function over their inputs while keeping those inputs private, but it requires active participation from all parties during computation.[4] zkML, by contrast, allows one party to prove computations to another party after the fact, without requiring the verifier to participate in the actual computation.

Technical Scope and Limitations

Current zkML implementations primarily focus on the inference phase of machine learning rather than training. This limitation stems from the computational intensity of both ML training and zero-knowledge proof generation.[5] Training large neural networks involves millions or billions of parameter updates across numerous iterations, making it computationally prohibitive to generate zero-knowledge proofs for each update with current technology. However, inference—the process of applying a trained model to new data—involves a single forward pass through the network, making it more amenable to zero-knowledge proof systems.

The mathematical foundation of zkML relies on converting floating-point arithmetic operations common in ML frameworks into finite field arithmetic suitable for zero-knowledge proofs. This conversion process, known as quantization, introduces potential accuracy trade-offs but enables the use of efficient polynomial commitment schemes and arithmetic circuits.[6] Modern zkML frameworks have developed sophisticated quantization techniques that minimize accuracy loss while maintaining computational efficiency in the zero-knowledge domain.

3.2 Workflow of zkML Systems

The zkML workflow encompasses several distinct phases, each presenting unique technical challenges and opportunities for optimization. Understanding this workflow is essential for grasping how abstract mathematical concepts translate into practical systems capable of proving real-world machine learning computations.

Phase 1: Model Preparation and Conversion

The zkML process begins with a trained machine learning model, typically developed using standard frameworks such as PyTorch or TensorFlow. This model must be converted into a format compatible with zero-knowledge proof systems—a process that involves several critical steps.

The first step involves exporting the model to the Open Neural Network Exchange (ONNX) format, an industry-standard intermediate representation that captures the computational graph of neural networks.[7] ONNX provides a framework-agnostic representation of ML models, enabling interoperability between different training frameworks and deployment environments. The ONNX representation includes the model's architecture, trained parameters (weights and biases), and the sequence of operations required for inference.

Following ONNX conversion, the model undergoes compilation into an arithmetic circuit suitable for zero-knowledge proofs. This compilation process involves mapping high-level ML operations—such as matrix multiplications, convolutions, and activation functions—onto basic arithmetic operations over finite fields.[8] The choice of finite field and the specific arithmetic circuit representation significantly impacts both the efficiency of proof generation and the accuracy of the final result.

// Example workflow using EZKL framework

1. Model Training (PyTorch/TensorFlow)

↓

2. ONNX Export

model.export_onnx("model.onnx")

↓

3. Circuit Compilation

ezkl.compile_circuit(model="model.onnx", settings="settings.json")

↓

4. Trusted Setup (if using zk-SNARKs)

ezkl.setup(circuit="circuit.json", srs="srs.json")

Phase 2: Quantization and Optimization

A critical aspect of the model conversion process involves quantization—the conversion of floating-point arithmetic to fixed-point or integer arithmetic compatible with finite field operations. Traditional ML models operate using 32-bit or 64-bit floating-point numbers, which provide high precision but are incompatible with the integer arithmetic required by most zero-knowledge proof systems.[9]

Modern zkML frameworks employ sophisticated quantization strategies that balance accuracy preservation with computational efficiency. These strategies include:

- **Static quantization**: Pre-computing quantization parameters based on calibration data
- **Dynamic quantization**: Adapting quantization parameters during inference
- **Mixed-precision approaches**: Using different precisions for different model components

The quantization process directly impacts both the accuracy of the final model and the complexity of the resulting arithmetic circuit. Higher precision generally yields better accuracy but requires more complex circuits and longer proof generation times.[10]

Phase 3: Witness Generation and Proof Creation

Once the model has been compiled into an arithmetic circuit, the actual proving process can begin. The prover executes the model on their private input data, generating what cryptographers term a "witness"—a complete trace of all intermediate values computed during the inference process.

The witness generation process involves:

1. **Input processing**: Converting the input data into the appropriate finite field representation
2. **Forward propagation**: Executing each layer of the neural network in sequence
3. **Constraint satisfaction**: Verifying that each operation satisfies the arithmetic circuit constraints
4. **Output extraction**: Producing the final prediction in both native and finite field formats

Following witness generation, the zero-knowledge proof is constructed using the chosen proof system (zk-SNARK, zk-STARK, or others). This process involves complex polynomial arithmetic and cryptographic operations that transform the witness into a succinct proof.[11]

Phase 4: Verification

The final phase involves verification of the zero-knowledge proof by the interested party. Verification in zkML systems typically requires:

- The zero-knowledge proof itself
- The public parameters of the proof system
- The model's public specification (architecture, but not weights)
- The claimed input-output pair (if public)

The verification process is designed to be computationally efficient, often requiring only milliseconds to verify proofs that took minutes or hours to generate. This asymmetry between proving and verification times is a key feature that enables practical deployment of zkML systems.[12]

3.3 Key Innovations

The practical realization of zkML has required numerous technical innovations spanning cryptography, machine learning, and system design. These innovations have transformed zkML from a theoretical possibility into a practical technology capable of handling realistic machine learning models.

Efficient Arithmetic Circuit Representations

One of the most significant challenges in zkML lies in efficiently representing complex ML operations as arithmetic circuits. Traditional approaches that directly translate each floating-point operation into circuit constraints resulted in prohibitively large circuits for any practical model. Modern zkML systems employ several innovative approaches to address this challenge:

Specialized Gadgets and Constraints: Contemporary zkML frameworks implement optimized "gadgets"—pre-designed circuit components for common ML operations such as matrix multiplication, convolution, and activation functions. These gadgets exploit the mathematical structure of ML operations to minimize the number of constraints required.[13] For example, a matrix multiplication gadget can leverage the inherent parallelism in vector dot products to reduce circuit complexity.

Lookup Tables for Non-linear Operations: Non-linear activation functions such as ReLU, sigmoid, and softmax pose particular challenges for arithmetic circuits. Recent innovations employ lookup tables to handle these operations efficiently, pre-computing function values for a discretized input domain and using table lookups instead of polynomial approximations.[14]

Advanced Proving Systems for ML

The adaptation of zero-knowledge proof systems specifically for machine learning has driven numerous cryptographic innovations:

Halo2 and Recursive Proofs: The Halo2 proving system, based on PLONK, offers several advantages for zkML applications, including elimination of trusted setup requirements and support for recursive proof composition. Recursive proofs enable the composition of multiple ML computations into a single proof, allowing for more complex model architectures and multi-stage inference pipelines.[15]

GKR-based Approaches: The Goldwasser-Kalai-Rothblum (GKR) protocol has proven particularly well-suited for the layered structure of neural networks. GKR treats the entire neural network as a layered arithmetic circuit and proves correctness using the sum-check protocol, offering potential efficiency advantages over traditional SNARK-based approaches.[16]

Handling Large Language Models and Transformers

The adaptation of zkML to modern transformer architectures and large language models represents a frontier of current research. These models present unique challenges due to their size, complexity, and the attention mechanisms that create non-local dependencies between inputs.

Recent work has demonstrated the feasibility of creating zero-knowledge proofs for transformer-based models, including distilled versions of GPT-2 and specialized attention mechanisms.[17] These implementations required innovative approaches to handle:

- **Self-attention mechanisms**: The quadratic complexity of attention operations required specialized circuit designs and optimization techniques

- **Large parameter spaces**: Models with millions or billions of parameters necessitated memory-efficient proof systems and parameter compression techniques
- **Sequence-to-sequence operations**: Variable-length inputs and outputs required dynamic circuit sizing and constraint generation

zkLLM: Verifiable Large Language Model Outputs

The emergence of large language models has created an urgent need for verifiable AI outputs, particularly given concerns about AI-generated misinformation and the authenticity of AI-created content. zkLLM represents the application of zero-knowledge proofs to prove that specific text was generated by a particular language model, potentially enabling verification of AI-generated content without revealing the model's weights or internal state.[18]

This capability has profound implications for content authenticity, AI safety, and intellectual property protection. News organizations could prove that articles were written by human journalists rather than AI, while AI companies could demonstrate the authenticity of their models' outputs without revealing proprietary information.

Optimizing Proof Generation Performance

Practical zkML deployment requires proof generation times that are acceptable for real-world applications. Several optimization strategies have emerged:

Parallel Proof Generation: Modern implementations exploit the inherent parallelism in neural network computations to accelerate proof generation across multiple processors or GPUs.[19]

Incremental Verification: For applications requiring multiple inferences with the same model, incremental verification techniques can amortize the cost of proof generation across multiple computations.

Hardware Acceleration: Specialized hardware for zero-knowledge proof generation, including FPGA and ASIC implementations, promise to dramatically reduce proof generation times and energy consumption.[20]

3.4 Decentralized zkML

The integration of zkML with blockchain technology and decentralized systems represents perhaps the most transformative application of this technology. Decentralized zkML enables trustless machine learning in environments where no single party can be trusted with sensitive data or model execution, opening new possibilities for privacy-preserving AI in decentralized applications.

The Oracle Problem and Off-chain Computation

Blockchain systems face a fundamental limitation known as the "oracle problem"—the difficulty of incorporating external data and computations into smart contracts in a trustless manner.[21] Traditional oracles require trust in centralized data providers, creating potential points of failure and manipulation. zkML offers a revolutionary solution by enabling complex machine learning computations to be performed off-chain while providing cryptographic guarantees that the results are correct.

In a zkML-enabled blockchain system, a smart contract can request that an external party perform machine learning inference on specified data using a designated model. The external party (prover) performs the computation and generates a zero-knowledge proof attesting to the correctness of their result. The smart contract can then verify this proof on-chain, gaining confidence in the result without needing to trust the prover or repeat the computation.[22]

This architecture offers several advantages:

- **Computational Scalability**: Complex ML models can be executed off-chain on specialized hardware while maintaining on-chain verifiability
- **Cost Efficiency**: The cost of proof verification is typically orders of

magnitude lower than re-executing the original computation

- **Privacy Preservation**: Sensitive input data and model parameters can remain private while still providing verifiable results

Decentralized Training and Model Updates

While current zkML implementations primarily focus on inference, emerging research explores the application of zero-knowledge proofs to distributed training scenarios. Decentralized training with zkML verification could enable multiple parties to collaboratively train models while maintaining privacy and ensuring the integrity of the training process.[23]

Consider a federated learning scenario where multiple hospitals wish to collaboratively train a diagnostic model without sharing patient data. zkML could enable each hospital to prove that their local training updates were computed correctly on legitimate data, without revealing any information about their patient population. The global model update could then incorporate these verified local updates, ensuring both privacy and correctness.

Smart Contract Integration and Automated Decision Making

The integration of zkML with smart contracts enables unprecedented automation and intelligence in decentralized applications. Smart contracts can incorporate sophisticated decision-making logic based on verified machine learning outputs, enabling applications such as:

Automated Risk Assessment: DeFi protocols can use zkML to implement sophisticated risk models for lending, trading, and liquidity provision. For example, a lending protocol could verify that a borrower's credit score was computed correctly using a specific model and blockchain transaction history, without revealing the details of the risk assessment algorithm.[24]

Dynamic Pricing Mechanisms: Automated market makers (AMMs) can use zkML to implement dynamic pricing strategies based on market conditions, order flow analysis, and risk metrics. The pricing algorithm can remain proprietary while providing cryptographic guarantees that prices were computed fairly.[25]

Verifiable Content Moderation: Decentralized social media platforms can use zkML to prove that content moderation decisions were made using specific, auditable models, addressing concerns about censorship and bias while maintaining the efficiency of automated moderation.

Blockchain-Native AI Models

An emerging paradigm involves deploying AI models that are native to blockchain environments from inception. These models are designed specifically for on-chain verification and can provide real-time intelligence for smart contracts and decentralized applications.

The Rocky Bot project exemplifies this approach, implementing an AI trading bot that generates zero-knowledge proofs for each trading decision.[26] The bot's training data, algorithm, and model weights are logged to the blockchain with cryptographic proofs, allowing users to verify that the bot's decisions follow its claimed strategy without revealing proprietary trading logic.

Cross-Chain AI and Interoperability

As the blockchain ecosystem becomes increasingly multi-chain, zkML enables AI models to operate across different blockchain networks while maintaining consistent verification standards. A model trained on one blockchain can generate proofs that are verifiable on other networks, enabling cross-chain AI applications and reducing the fragmentation of decentralized AI services.[27]

Projects like Polyhedra Network's EXPchain demonstrate this vision by creating specialized blockchain infrastructure for zkML applications, featuring hardware acceleration and optimized verification protocols for AI workloads.[28]

Economic Models and Incentive Alignment

Decentralized zkML requires careful consideration of economic incentives to ensure sustainable operation. The computational cost of generating zero-knowledge proofs must be balanced against the value provided to users, while ensuring that provers are adequately compensated for their computational resources.

Several economic models have emerged:

Proof-as-a-Service: Specialized providers offer zkML proof generation services, competing on cost, speed, and reliability **Staking and Slashing**: Proof providers stake tokens that can be slashed if they provide incorrect proofs, aligning economic incentives with correct behavior **Verifiable Compute Networks**: Decentralized networks of compute providers offer zkML services with built-in dispute resolution and quality assurance mechanisms

Future Implications and Societal Impact

The emergence of decentralized zkML has profound implications for the future of AI deployment and governance. By enabling verifiable, privacy-preserving AI in trustless environments, zkML could:

- **Democratize AI Access**: Reduce reliance on centralized AI providers and enable broader access to AI capabilities
- **Enhance AI Accountability**: Provide cryptographic guarantees about AI behavior and decision-making processes
- **Enable Privacy-Preserving AI**: Allow sensitive data to be used for AI applications without compromising privacy
- **Support AI Regulation**: Provide technical infrastructure for verifiable compliance with AI governance frameworks

The convergence of zero-knowledge proofs, machine learning, and blockchain technology represents a fundamental shift toward more trustworthy, transparent, and decentralized AI systems. As zkML technology continues to mature, it promises to reshape how we think about AI deployment, data privacy, and computational trust in an increasingly digital world.

Conclusion

The emergence of zkML represents a paradigmatic shift in how we approach machine learning deployment and verification. By combining the mathematical rigor of zero-knowledge proofs with the practical power of machine learning, zkML addresses fundamental challenges in AI trustworthiness, privacy, and verifiability. From enabling verifiable inference on private data to powering sophisticated decentralized applications, zkML has evolved from theoretical concept to practical technology with far-reaching implications.

The innovations discussed in this chapter—from efficient arithmetic circuit representations to decentralized training protocols—demonstrate the rapid pace of development in this field. As zkML continues to mature, it promises to unlock new possibilities for privacy-preserving AI, trustless computation, and decentralized intelligence that could fundamentally reshape our digital infrastructure.

The next chapter will examine the tools and frameworks that make these innovations accessible to practitioners, exploring how developers and researchers can leverage existing zkML infrastructure to build the next generation of verifiable AI applications.

Footnotes

[1] Kang, Daniel, et al. "ZKML: An Optimizing System for ML Inference in Zero-Knowledge Proofs." *Proceedings of the Nineteenth European Conference on Computer Systems* (2024). https://dl.acm.org/doi/10.1145/3627703.3650088

[2] Chen, Bing-Jyue, et al. "A Survey of Zero-Knowledge Proof Based Verifiable Machine Learning." *arXiv preprint arXiv:2502.18535* (2025). https://arxiv.org/abs/2502.18535

[3] Worldcoin. "An introduction to zero-knowledge machine learning (ZKML)." *Worldcoin Blog* (December 20, 2023). https://world.org/blog/engineering/intro-to-zkml

[4] Xing, Zhibo, et al. "Zero-Knowledge Proof-based Verifiable Decentralized Machine Learning in Communication Network: A Comprehensive Survey." *arXiv preprint arXiv:2310.14848* (2025). https://arxiv.org/abs/2310.14848

[5] Spectral Finance. "The State of Zero-Knowledge Machine Learning (zkML)." *Spectral Blog* (March 25, 2024). https://blog.spectral.finance/the-state-of-zero-knowledge-machine-learning-zkml/

[6] NP Labs. "zkML: Tradeoffs in accuracy vs. proving cost." *NP Labs Engineering* (July 24, 2024). https://np.engineering/posts/zkml-tradeoffs/

[7] Polyhedra Network. "zkPyTorch: Verifiable PyTorch with Zero-Knowledge Proofs." *Polyhedra Blog* (June 5, 2025). https://blog.polyhedra.network/zkpytorch/

[8] Kersic, Vid. "Demystifying ZKML." *Medium* (November 27, 2023). https://medium.com/@vid.kersic/demystifying-zkml-0f3dff7194b9

[9] Chen, Bing-Jyue, et al. "ZKML: An Optimizing System for ML Inference in Zero-Knowledge Proofs." *ResearchGate* (April 22, 2024). https://www.researchgate.net/publication/379999064_ZKML_An_Optimizing_System_for_ML_Inference_in_Zero-Knowled

[10] Credio Documentation. "Zero-Knowledge Machine Learning (zkML)." *Credio Network.* https://docs.credio.network/docs/Credio/ZKML/zero-knowledge-machine-learning

[11] Kinic AI. "JOLT Atlas Reaching For SOTA In Zero Knowledge Machine Learning (zkML)." *Kinic AI Blog.* https://www.kinic.io/blog/joltx-reaching-for-sota-in-zero-knowledge-machine-learning-zkml

[12] Ledger Academy. "Zero-Knowledge Machine Learning (zkML)." *Ledger* (March 25, 2025). https://www.ledger.com/academy/glossary/zero-knowledge-machine-learning-zkml

[13] Zkrypto Inc. "ZKML: An Optimizing System for ML Inference in Zero-Knowledge Proofs." *Medium* (November 23, 2024). https://zkrypto.medium.com/zkml-an-optimizing-system-for-ml-inference-in-zero-knowledge-proofs-f9e4cafbefbe

[14] Chen, Bing-Jyue, et al. "A Survey of Zero-Knowledge Proof Based Verifiable Machine Learning." *arXiv HTML* (February 25, 2025). https://arxiv.org/html/2502.18535v1

[15] Spectral Finance. "The State of Zero-Knowledge Machine Learning (zkML)."

[16] Kinic AI. "JOLT Atlas Reaching For SOTA In Zero Knowledge Machine Learning (zkML)."

[17] Kang, Daniel, et al. "ZKML: An Optimizing System for ML Inference in Zero-Knowledge Proofs."

[18] Worldcoin. "An introduction to zero-knowledge machine learning (ZKML)."

[19] Zhang, Tiancheng, et al. "Zero-Knowledge Proofs of Training for Deep Neural Networks." *Proceedings of the 2024 ACM SIGSAC Conference on Computer and Communications Security* (2024). https://dl.acm.org/doi/10.1145/3658644.3670316

[20] NP Labs. "zkML: Tradeoffs in accuracy vs. proving cost."

[21] OpenGradient. "A Gentle Introduction to zkML." *Medium* (July 16, 2025). https://opengradient.medium.com/a-gentle-introduction-to-zkml-8049a0e10a04

[22] Mina Protocol. "Zero-knowledge Machine Learning on the Mina Protocol." *Mina Blog* (October 29, 2024). https://minaprotocol.com/blog/zero-knowledge-machine-learning-on-the-mina-protocol

[23] Xing, Zhibo, et al. "Zero-Knowledge Proof-based Verifiable Decentralized Machine Learning in Communication Network: A Comprehensive Survey."

[24] Imperii Partners. "The Rise of zkML and Decentralized AI." *Imperii Partners Blog* (March 25, 2024). https://imperiipartners.com/the-emergence-of-ai-application-in-crypto/

[25] DEV Community. "ZKML: Bringing Verifiable and Trustless ML to the Masses." *DEV* (April 21, 2024). https://dev.to/gssakash/zkml-bringing-verifiable-and-trustless-ml-to-the-masses-2a38

[26] Worldcoin. "An introduction to zero-knowledge machine learning (ZKML)."

[27] Vara Network. "ZKML: Empowering Privacy on Vara Network." *Vara Network Documentation.* https://wiki.vara.network/docs/examples/Infra/zkml

[28] Polyhedra Network. "zkPyTorch: Verifiable PyTorch with Zero-Knowledge Proofs."

Chapter 4: Tools, Frameworks, and Implementations

The practical deployment of zero-knowledge machine learning (zkML) systems depends critically on the availability of robust tools, frameworks, and implementations that can bridge the gap between theoretical concepts and real-world applications. As the field has matured, a diverse ecosystem of development tools has emerged, each offering unique approaches to the fundamental challenge of converting machine learning models into zero-knowledge proof circuits. This chapter provides a comprehensive examination of the current landscape of zkML tools, from high-level frameworks that abstract away circuit complexity to low-level libraries that offer fine-grained control over proof generation.

The evolution of zkML tooling has been driven by the need to make zero-knowledge proofs accessible to machine learning practitioners who may lack deep expertise in cryptography. Early implementations required developers to manually construct arithmetic circuits for even simple computations, creating a significant barrier to adoption. Today's frameworks address this challenge by providing automated compilation pipelines that can transform standard ML models into zkSNARK-compatible representations, dramatically reducing the technical overhead required to implement privacy-preserving AI systems.

4.1 zkML Libraries and Frameworks

The foundation of practical zkML development rests on specialized libraries and frameworks that automate the complex process of converting machine learning models into zero-knowledge proof circuits. These tools represent years of research and engineering effort to make zkML accessible to a broader community of developers and researchers.

EZKL: Comprehensive ML-to-ZK Pipeline

EZKL (pronounced "easy-kelly") stands as one of the most mature and widely-adopted frameworks for zkML development[1]. Developed by Zkonduit, EZKL provides an end-to-end pipeline for generating zero-knowledge proofs of deep learning model execution, supporting popular frameworks including PyTorch, TensorFlow, and scikit-learn. The framework's design philosophy emphasizes ease of use while maintaining the flexibility required for complex ML applications.

The EZKL workflow follows a standardized process that begins with exporting trained models to the Open Neural Network Exchange (ONNX) format[2]. This format-agnostic approach enables EZKL to work with models trained in virtually any major machine learning framework. The conversion process involves several critical steps: model quantization to handle the integer arithmetic required by zk-SNARKs, circuit generation using the Halo2 proving system, and proof generation that can be verified both off-chain and on-chain through automatically generated Solidity verifier contracts.

Performance benchmarks demonstrate EZKL's practical viability for real-world applications. The framework can prove an MNIST-sized model in approximately 6 seconds using 1.1GB of RAM[3], representing significant improvements over earlier zkML implementations. For more complex models, EZKL has successfully generated proofs for ImageNet-scale vision models, though with correspondingly higher computational requirements. The framework's memory efficiency has proven particularly noteworthy, with benchmarking studies showing EZKL using 63.95% less memory than competing frameworks like Orion and 98.13% less than RISC Zero[4].

EZKL's architecture incorporates several optimization techniques to improve proving efficiency. The framework implements automated quantization calibration, which determines optimal precision levels for converting floating-point operations to integer arithmetic while minimizing accuracy loss. This process is crucial because zk-SNARK circuits operate over finite fields, requiring all computations to be expressed as arithmetic operations on integers. The calibration process uses representative input data to determine the scaling factors that preserve model accuracy while enabling efficient circuit representation.

Recent developments in EZKL have expanded support for advanced model architectures, including transformer-based networks and recurrent neural networks. The framework now includes specialized templates for attention mechanisms, a critical component for large language models and modern computer vision architectures. Additionally, EZKL has introduced support for batch verification, enabling multiple proofs to be verified simultaneously with improved efficiency.

zkml Framework: Scaling to Realistic Models

The zkml framework, developed by Daniel Kang and his research team, represents a significant advancement in scaling zero-knowledge proofs to realistic machine learning models[5]. Built on the foundation of rigorous academic research, this framework was the first to demonstrate zkSNARK proofs for ImageNet-scale models, achieving 92.4% accuracy while providing cryptographic guarantees about model execution.

The framework's architecture is built around an optimizing compiler that transforms TensorFlow models into Halo2 zero-knowledge proof circuits. This compiler incorporates several key innovations that enable scalability to large models. First, it implements efficient constraint gadgets for fundamental machine learning operations, including matrix multiplication, convolution, and non-linear activation functions. These gadgets are optimized specifically for the constraint systems used in zk-SNARKs, minimizing the number of constraints required for each operation.

A critical component of the zkml framework is its Circuit Layout Optimizer, which automatically determines the optimal arrangement of constraints to minimize proving time and memory usage[6]. This optimizer considers the trade-offs between different constraint representations and selects configurations that balance computational efficiency with resource consumption. The optimization process can achieve up to 131% performance improvements compared to naive circuit constructions, making the difference between practical and impractical zkML applications.

The framework has demonstrated remarkable scalability across diverse model architectures. Beyond computer vision models, zkml has successfully generated proofs for recommendation systems, including a production-scale model used by Twitter for content recommendation. This achievement is particularly significant because recommendation models often involve complex sparse operations and embedding lookups that are challenging to represent efficiently in arithmetic circuits.

Performance evaluations of the zkml framework reveal the computational intensity of realistic zkML applications. Proving an ImageNet model with non-trivial accuracy requires approximately 45 minutes on high-end hardware, while simpler models can be proven in under 4 minutes[7]. These benchmarks underscore both the progress made in zkML tooling and the continued need for optimization, particularly as the field moves toward even larger models like GPT-scale language models.

Specialized Frameworks and Emerging Tools

The zkML ecosystem continues to evolve with specialized frameworks targeting specific use cases and optimization strategies. Modulus Labs has developed proprietary zkML infrastructure focused on on-chain verifiable AI, though much of their work remains closed-source[8]. Their research has contributed significantly to understanding the computational costs of zkML, providing detailed benchmarks that guide the development of more efficient systems.

Several academic projects have contributed important tools to the zkML landscape. The ZEN quantization scheme, developed by researchers at leading universities, introduces novel optimization techniques specifically designed for zero-knowledge circuits[9]. ZEN incorporates sign-bit grouping and remainder-based verification optimizations that achieve up to 73.9x savings in R1CS constraints for convolution operations compared to standard quantization approaches.

The diversity of frameworks reflects the varied requirements of different zkML applications. While some prioritize ease of use for rapid prototyping, others focus on maximal performance for production deployments. This ecosystem approach has proven beneficial for the field's development, enabling experimentation with different architectural approaches and optimization strategies.

4.2 Circuit Compilers and Provers

The translation of high-level machine learning operations into arithmetic circuits suitable for zero-knowledge proofs requires sophisticated compilation tools. These circuit compilers and proving systems form the foundational layer upon which zkML frameworks operate, determining the efficiency and capabilities of the entire system.

Circom: Domain-Specific Circuit Language

Circom represents a paradigm shift in zero-knowledge proof development, providing a domain-specific language specifically designed for constructing arithmetic circuits[10]. Developed by the Iden3 team, Circom abstracts away much of the complexity involved in creating constraint systems while maintaining the flexibility required for complex applications like machine learning.

The Circom language is built around the concept of templates and components, which enable modular circuit construction. Templates define reusable circuit patterns, while components instantiate these templates with specific parameters. This architecture proves particularly valuable for zkML applications, where common operations like matrix multiplication and activation functions can be implemented once and reused across different model architectures.

Circom's compilation process generates three critical outputs that enable zero-knowledge proof generation. First, it produces an R1CS (Rank-1 Constraint System) file that encodes the arithmetic constraints defining the circuit. Second, it generates WebAssembly and C++ programs that efficiently compute witness values—the secret inputs and intermediate values that satisfy the constraints. Finally, it creates the infrastructure needed to interface with proving systems like snarkjs for proof generation and verification[11].

The language's syntax is designed to be accessible to developers familiar with conventional programming languages while enforcing the constraints necessary for zero-knowledge proof systems. Variables in Circom, called signals, can be classified as input, output, or intermediate values. The language enforces strict rules about signal assignment and constraint generation, helping developers avoid common pitfalls that could compromise the security or correctness of their circuits.

For machine learning applications, Circom's template system has proven particularly valuable. Developers can create templates for common ML operations—such as ReLU activation functions, pooling layers, or attention mechanisms—and reuse these components across different model architectures. This modularity significantly reduces the development time required to implement zkML systems and helps ensure consistency in circuit implementations.

The circomlib-ml library extends Circom's capabilities specifically for machine learning applications[12]. This specialized library provides pre-built templates for neural network layers including convolutional layers, dense layers, and various activation functions. The library addresses the unique challenges of representing floating-point machine learning operations in the integer arithmetic required by zk-SNARKs, implementing carefully designed scaling strategies to preserve numerical precision.

One of the most significant challenges addressed by circomlib-ml is the quantization process required to convert floating-point neural networks to integer arithmetic. The library implements sophisticated scaling strategies that maintain model accuracy while enabling efficient circuit representation. For example, weights in convolutional layers might be scaled by 10^9 for precision, requiring corresponding adjustments to biases and activation functions to maintain mathematical correctness[13].

libsnark: Low-Level zkSNARK Operations

At the foundational level of the zkML stack lies libsnark, a comprehensive C++ library that implements the core cryptographic primitives required for zk-SNARK proof systems[14]. Developed by the SCIPR Lab, libsnark provides the mathematical machinery that powers many higher-level zkML frameworks, offering both preprocessing and non-preprocessing zkSNARK implementations.

The library's architecture is designed around templates that efficiently support operations on multiple elliptic curves simultaneously. This flexibility is crucial for zkML applications, where different elliptic curves may offer varying trade-offs between security, efficiency, and compatibility with existing blockchain infrastructure. The template-based design also enables optimization for specific hardware architectures, supporting both CPU and GPU acceleration strategies.

libsnark implements several important zkSNARK constructions, including the widely-used Groth16 protocol and more recent developments like the non-preprocessing systems. For zkML applications, the choice of proving system can significantly impact performance characteristics. Groth16 offers extremely small proof sizes and fast verification but requires a trusted setup ceremony for each circuit. Alternative systems like PLONK provide universal setup but may have different performance trade-offs for specific ML workloads.

The library includes two distinct APIs for constraint system construction: gadgetlib1 and gadgetlib2. These libraries provide different levels of abstraction for building arithmetic circuits, with gadgetlib1 offering more direct control over constraint generation and gadgetlib2 providing a higher-level interface that simplifies development for complex applications. Many zkML frameworks build upon these constraint libraries, using them as the foundation for implementing machine learning operations in arithmetic circuits.

Performance optimization in libsnark requires careful attention to several factors. The library's proving algorithms are computationally intensive, with complexity that scales roughly linearly with the number of constraints in the circuit. For zkML applications, which often involve millions of constraints for realistic models, these computational requirements can become prohibitive without proper optimization. The library provides several strategies for managing this complexity, including constraint batching and optimized finite field arithmetic.

Bulletproofs: Transparent Zero-Knowledge Arguments

Bulletproofs represent an alternative approach to zero-knowledge proof construction that offers several advantages for specific zkML applications[15]. Unlike zk-SNARKs, Bulletproofs require no trusted setup, making them particularly attractive for applications where trust assumptions must be minimized. This transparency comes at the cost of larger proof sizes and longer verification times, creating trade-offs that must be carefully considered for each application.

The mathematical foundation of Bulletproofs rests on inner product arguments and Pedersen commitments, providing a construction that is both elegant and efficient for certain types of computations. For machine learning applications, Bulletproofs excel at range proofs—demonstrating that values lie within specified bounds without revealing the values themselves. This capability proves valuable for privacy-preserving machine learning scenarios where model outputs or intermediate computations must be proven to be well-formed without disclosure.

Bulletproofs support aggregation, enabling multiple range proofs to be combined into a single, compact argument. This feature is particularly relevant for zkML applications involving multiple model predictions or batch processing scenarios. The aggregation property means that proving statements about multiple values requires only logarithmic additional space compared to a single proof, providing significant efficiency gains for batch operations.

The construction of Bulletproofs for arbitrary arithmetic circuits requires more complex protocols than simple range proofs, but recent research has demonstrated the feasibility of this approach for machine learning applications. The lack of trusted setup makes Bulletproofs particularly attractive for decentralized scenarios where participants may be unwilling to trust a centralized setup ceremony.

Implementation of Bulletproofs for zkML requires careful attention to the specific characteristics of machine learning computations. The proof system works most efficiently with computations that can be expressed as inner products or linear combinations, making it well-suited for certain types of neural network operations. However, non-linear activation functions and complex control flow can be more challenging to implement efficiently in Bulletproofs compared to zk-SNARKs.

4.3 Optimization Techniques

The computational intensity of zero-knowledge proof generation necessitates aggressive optimization strategies to make zkML practical for real-world applications. These optimizations span multiple levels of the system stack, from algorithmic improvements to specialized hardware acceleration.

Hardware Acceleration Strategies

The move toward hardware acceleration for zero-knowledge proofs mirrors the evolution seen in cryptocurrency mining and deep learning, where specialized hardware has become essential for competitive performance[16]. For zkML applications, hardware acceleration focuses on optimizing the mathematical operations that dominate proof generation time: multi-scalar multiplication (MSM), number-theoretic transforms (NTT), and finite field arithmetic.

Graphics Processing Units (GPUs) have emerged as the most accessible platform for zkML acceleration. Modern GPUs provide massive parallelism that maps well to the embarrassingly parallel nature of many zkSNARK operations. MSM operations, which can account for 70-80% of proving time in many zkML applications, benefit significantly from GPU acceleration. Benchmarks demonstrate speedups of 131% for MSM operations when moving from CPU to optimized GPU implementations[17].

The CUDA ecosystem has proven particularly valuable for zkML acceleration, with libraries like Sppark providing highly optimized implementations of cryptographic primitives. These implementations leverage GPU-specific optimizations like shared memory hierarchies and warp-level operations to maximize throughput. For zkML applications, GPU acceleration can reduce proving times from hours to minutes for realistic model sizes, making the difference between research curiosities and practical applications.

Field-Programmable Gate Arrays (FPGAs) offer a different optimization approach that trades development complexity for potentially superior performance characteristics[18]. FPGA implementations can be optimized down to the level of individual arithmetic operations, enabling optimizations that are impossible with software-only approaches. Recent research has demonstrated FPGA implementations that achieve significant performance improvements over GPU solutions for specific zkSNARK operations.

The OPTIMSM project represents a significant advancement in FPGA-based acceleration for zero-knowledge proofs[19]. This implementation introduces novel iteration techniques that decouple bucket requirements from window sizes in the Pippenger MSM algorithm, resulting in up to 12.77x speedups compared to previous FPGA implementations. Such optimizations are crucial for zkML applications, where MSM operations often dominate computational costs.

The choice between GPU and FPGA acceleration involves several trade-offs. GPUs offer shorter development cycles and broader availability, particularly given the large number of GPUs made available by the transition of Ethereum from proof-of-work to proof-of-stake. FPGAs provide superior power efficiency and lower latency but require specialized development expertise and longer development cycles. For production zkML deployments, the choice often depends on the specific performance requirements and available development resources.

Application-Specific Integrated Circuits (ASICs) represent the ultimate optimization approach but require substantial investment and longer development cycles. For zkML applications, ASIC development faces the additional challenge of rapidly evolving algorithms and proof systems. The high cost and long development times of ASICs make them viable only for very high-volume applications or scenarios where maximum efficiency is critical.

Model Compression and Quantization

The computational cost of zkML proofs scales roughly linearly with model complexity, making model compression techniques essential for practical deployments. These techniques reduce model size and computational requirements while attempting to preserve accuracy, directly translating to more efficient zero-knowledge proof generation.

Quantization represents the most widely applicable compression technique for zkML applications[20]. The process involves reducing the precision of model weights and activations from 32-bit floating-point representations to lower-precision formats like 8-bit or even 1-bit integers. For zkML, quantization serves a dual purpose: reducing computational requirements and facilitating the conversion to integer arithmetic required by zk-SNARKs.

Post-training quantization techniques have proven particularly valuable for zkML applications because they can be applied to pre-trained models without requiring access to training data or computational resources for retraining. These techniques analyze the distribution of weights and activations in the trained model to determine optimal quantization parameters. Modern post-training quantization methods can achieve 3-4x model compression with minimal accuracy loss, directly translating to similar improvements in zkML proving efficiency.

Quantization-aware training represents a more sophisticated approach that incorporates quantization effects during the training process itself. This technique typically achieves better accuracy-compression trade-offs than post-training methods but requires access to training data and computational resources for retraining. For zkML applications, quantization-aware training can be particularly valuable because it enables optimization for the specific quantization schemes required by different proving systems.

The ZEN quantization scheme introduces optimizations specifically designed for zero-knowledge circuits[21]. This approach implements sign-bit grouping and remainder-based verification techniques that are particularly efficient in R1CS constraint systems. ZEN achieves up to 73.9x reductions in constraint counts for convolution operations compared to standard quantization approaches, demonstrating the value of co-designing quantization schemes with the underlying proving systems.

Pruning techniques remove unnecessary connections or parameters from neural networks, reducing both model size and computational requirements. Unstructured pruning removes individual weights based on magnitude or other importance metrics, while structured pruning removes entire neurons, channels, or layers. For zkML applications, structured pruning often provides better efficiency gains because it reduces the overall circuit complexity rather than just setting weights to zero.

The interaction between pruning and zero-knowledge circuits requires careful consideration. While unstructured pruning can significantly reduce the number of non-zero parameters, the resulting sparse models may not translate directly to constraint reductions in arithmetic circuits. Structured pruning, which removes entire computational units, typically provides more direct benefits for zkML applications by reducing the overall circuit size.

Knowledge distillation offers another approach to model compression that can be particularly effective for zkML applications. This technique trains a smaller "student" model to mimic the behavior of a larger "teacher" model, often achieving comparable accuracy with significantly reduced computational requirements. For zkML, knowledge distillation enables the use of simpler model architectures that are more amenable to efficient circuit representation.

Advanced Circuit Optimizations

Beyond hardware acceleration and model compression, several circuit-level optimization techniques can significantly improve zkML performance. These optimizations work at the level of constraint systems and arithmetic circuits, requiring deep understanding of both machine learning computations and zero-knowledge proof systems.

Constraint optimization focuses on reducing the number and complexity of arithmetic constraints required to represent machine learning operations. For example, ReLU activation functions, which are conceptually simple, require complex constraint representations in arithmetic circuits. Recent research has developed polynomial approximations and other techniques that reduce the constraint overhead for common activation functions while maintaining sufficient accuracy for machine learning applications.

Lookup table optimizations represent another important direction for circuit optimization. Many machine learning operations, particularly activation functions and normalization operations, can be approximated using pre-computed lookup tables. In zero-knowledge circuits, these tables can be implemented using specialized constraint gadgets that reduce the overall circuit complexity compared to computing these functions directly.

Batch processing techniques enable multiple model inferences to be proven simultaneously, amortizing the fixed costs of proof setup across multiple computations. This approach is particularly valuable for applications that require proving many similar computations, such as batch image classification or recommendation systems. Batch processing can achieve significant efficiency gains, though it requires careful circuit design to ensure that the batching doesn't compromise the security properties of the zero-knowledge proof.

4.4 Benchmarks and Evaluations

Rigorous benchmarking and evaluation frameworks are essential for understanding the practical capabilities and limitations of zkML systems. These benchmarks provide the empirical foundation for comparing different approaches and guiding optimization efforts.

Performance Metrics and Methodologies

The evaluation of zkML systems requires careful consideration of multiple performance dimensions that collectively determine practical viability. Proving time represents the most fundamental metric, measuring the duration required to generate a zero-knowledge proof for a given model and input. This metric directly impacts user experience and determines the feasibility of real-time applications.

Memory usage during proof generation represents another critical constraint, particularly for deployment on resource-limited systems. zkML proof generation can require gigabytes of RAM for realistic models, making memory efficiency crucial for practical deployments. Benchmarking studies consistently measure peak memory consumption during the proving process to understand resource requirements.

Proof size affects both storage and transmission costs, particularly important for blockchain applications where on-chain storage is expensive. Different proving systems offer varying trade-offs between proving time and proof size, with systems like Groth16 producing extremely compact proofs while others like STARKs generate larger proofs in exchange for other benefits.

Verification time determines how quickly proofs can be checked, affecting both off-chain and on-chain verification scenarios. For blockchain applications, verification time directly impacts gas costs and transaction throughput. Most modern zkSNARK systems achieve verification times measured in milliseconds, but these can vary significantly based on circuit complexity and implementation details.

Accuracy preservation represents a unique challenge for zkML benchmarking. The quantization and approximation techniques required for efficient zero-knowledge circuits can introduce accuracy degradation compared to the original floating-point models. Benchmarking frameworks must carefully measure this accuracy impact to ensure that optimization efforts don't compromise model utility.

Comparative Framework Analysis

Recent comprehensive benchmarking studies have provided valuable insights into the relative performance of different zkML frameworks[22]. The EZKL benchmarking study compared three major frameworks—EZKL, Orion, and RISC Zero—across multiple model types and performance metrics, revealing significant differences in efficiency and capabilities.

The benchmarking methodology focused on four standard model types: linear regression, random forest classification, support vector machine classification, and tree ensemble regression. This selection enables fair comparison across frameworks while covering a representative range of machine learning algorithms. The benchmarks measured both proving time and memory usage across these model types.

Results demonstrated substantial performance differences between frameworks. EZKL consistently achieved the lowest memory usage, requiring 63.95% less memory than Orion and 98.13% less than RISC Zero on average. These differences reflect fundamental architectural choices in how the frameworks implement circuit generation and proof construction.

Proving time comparisons revealed more nuanced trade-offs. While EZKL generally achieved competitive proving times, the optimal framework choice depended on the specific model type and size. Some frameworks demonstrated particular efficiency for certain classes of models, highlighting the importance of matching framework capabilities to application requirements.

The benchmarking studies also revealed significant differences in setup complexity and developer experience across frameworks. Some frameworks required extensive manual configuration and parameter tuning, while others provided more automated workflows. These usability factors can be as important as raw performance for determining practical adoption.

Accuracy preservation varied significantly across frameworks, with some demonstrating better tolerance for the quantization effects inherent in zkML systems. Frameworks that provided more configurable quantization schemes generally achieved better accuracy-efficiency trade-offs, though at the cost of increased complexity for developers.

Hardware Performance Scaling

Understanding how zkML performance scales across different hardware configurations is crucial for deployment planning and cost optimization. Benchmarking studies have examined performance across CPU-optimized, memory-optimized, and GPU-accelerated systems to characterize these scaling behaviors[23].

CPU performance scaling generally follows predictable patterns, with proving time scaling roughly linearly with the number of cores for parallelizable operations. However, memory bandwidth often becomes the limiting factor for large models, making memory-optimized systems more cost-effective than CPU-optimized configurations for many zkML workloads.

GPU acceleration provides dramatic performance improvements for suitable workloads, with speedups of 10-100x common for MSM-dominated computations. However, not all zkML operations benefit equally from GPU acceleration, and the optimal GPU configuration depends on the specific characteristics of the model and framework being used.

Memory scaling characteristics reveal important deployment considerations. zkML applications often require substantially more memory than traditional machine learning inference, with memory requirements scaling super-linearly with model complexity. This scaling behavior has important implications for cloud deployment costs and hardware selection.

The benchmarking results provide concrete guidance for hardware selection and deployment optimization. For development and experimentation, mid-range GPUs provide good price-performance characteristics. For production deployments, high-memory GPU instances or FPGA-based solutions may offer better long-term economics depending on the specific application requirements.

Emerging Benchmarking Initiatives

The zkML community has recognized the need for standardized benchmarking frameworks that enable fair comparison across systems and track progress over time. Several initiatives have emerged to address this need, each focusing on different aspects of zkML performance and capabilities.

The ZK-Bench project provides a comprehensive framework for benchmarking zero-knowledge proof systems across multiple dimensions[24]. While not specifically focused on machine learning, this framework provides important infrastructure for evaluating the cryptographic primitives that underlie zkML systems. The framework emphasizes reproducibility and standardization, enabling consistent comparison across different implementations and optimization approaches.

BrainBench represents a specialized benchmarking initiative focused specifically on zkML frameworks[25]. This platform extends existing benchmarking methodologies to include additional metrics relevant to machine learning applications, such as accuracy preservation and model architecture support. The platform provides automated benchmarking infrastructure that enables continuous evaluation as frameworks evolve.

Community-driven benchmarking efforts have proven particularly valuable for identifying optimization opportunities and tracking ecosystem progress. These initiatives often reveal performance gaps and inspire targeted optimization efforts from framework developers. The collaborative nature of these benchmarks also helps establish common standards and best practices across the zkML community.

The evolution of benchmarking frameworks reflects the maturing zkML ecosystem. Early benchmarks focused primarily on basic functionality and proof generation times. Modern benchmarks incorporate more sophisticated metrics that reflect real-world deployment requirements, including accuracy preservation, memory efficiency, and developer experience factors.

Future benchmarking initiatives will likely incorporate more sophisticated evaluation criteria as zkML applications become more complex and demanding. Areas of particular interest include support for larger models, efficiency with different model architectures, and integration with existing machine learning infrastructure and workflows.

Footnotes:

[1] Zkonduit, "EZKL GitHub Repository," GitHub, accessed January 2025, https://github.com/zkonduit/ezkl.

[2] Spectral, "Zero-Knowledge Machine Learning (zkML)," Spectral Documentation, accessed January 2025.

[3] Justin McAfee, "zkML: Evolving the Intelligence of Smart Contracts Through Zero-Knowledge Cryptography," 1kxnetwork Medium, February 17, 2024.

[4] EZKL Team, "Benchmarking ZKML Frameworks," EZKL Blog, accessed January 2025.

[5] Daniel Kang et al., "ZKML: An Optimizing System for ML Inference in Zero-Knowledge Proofs," Proceedings of the Nineteenth European Conference on Computer Systems, 2024.

[6] Daniel Kang, "Open-sourcing zkml: Trustless Machine Learning for All," Daniel Kang Blog, April 3, 2023.

[7] Daniel Kang, "Scaling Trustless DNN Inference with Zero-Knowledge Proofs," ZKProof Standards, September 18, 2023.

[8] Elena Burger, "Checks and balances: Machine learning and zero-knowledge proofs," a16z Crypto, April 5, 2023.

[9] "A Survey of Zero-Knowledge Proof Based Verifiable Machine Learning," arXiv preprint arXiv:2502.18535, February 25, 2025.

[10] Marta Bellés-Muñoz et al., "Circom: A Circuit Description Language for Building Zero-Knowledge Applications," IEEE Transactions on Dependable and Secure Computing, 2022.

[11] "Zero-Knowledge Proofs with Circom: A domain-specific language purpose," ZKP Labs, accessed January 2025.

[12] socathie, "circomlib-ml: Circom Circuits Library for Machine Learning," GitHub, accessed January 2025.

[13] drCathieSo, "ZKML: Bridging AI/ML and Web3 with Zero-Knowledge Proofs," Privacy & Scaling Explorations, accessed January 2025.

[14] SCIPR Lab, "libsnark: C++ library for zkSNARKs," GitHub, accessed January 2025.

[15] Benedikt Bünz et al., "Bulletproofs: Short Proofs for Confidential Transactions and More," Stanford Applied Cryptography Group, 2017.

[16] Ingonyama, "Hardware Review: GPUs, FPGAs and Zero Knowledge Proofs," Ingonyama Blog, accessed January 2025.

[17] Omer Shlomovits, "Revisiting Paradigm 'Hardware Acceleration for Zero Knowledge Proofs'," Medium, September 19, 2023.

[18] Paradigm, "Hardware Acceleration for Zero Knowledge Proofs," Paradigm Blog, April 13, 2022.

[19] Xander Pottier et al., "OPTIMSM: FPGA hardware accelerator for Zero-Knowledge MSM," Cryptology ePrint Archive, November 7, 2024.

[20] SoftServe, "Deep Learning Model Compression and Optimization," SoftServe Blog, October 14, 2021.

[21] "A Survey of Zero-Knowledge Proof Based Verifiable Machine Learning," arXiv preprint arXiv:2502.18535, February 25, 2025.

[22] EZKL Team, "Benchmarking ZKML Frameworks," EZKL Blog, accessed January 2025.

[23] Max Kobelt et al., "A Benchmark for Different Implementations of Zero-Knowledge Proof Systems," ResearchGate, December 17, 2023.

[24] "zk-Bench: A Toolset for Comparative Evaluation and Performance Benchmarking of SNARKs," SpringerLink, 2023.

[25] Inference Labs, "BrainBench," BrainBench Platform, accessed January 2025.

Chapter 5: Applications of zkML

Zero-Knowledge Machine Learning (zkML) represents a paradigm shift in how artificial intelligence systems can be deployed across sensitive domains without compromising privacy or computational integrity. As organizations increasingly recognize the value of AI-driven insights while grappling with stringent data protection regulations and trust requirements, zkML emerges as a transformative technology that bridges the gap between utility and privacy. This chapter examines the practical applications of zkML across four critical domains: healthcare and biomedical applications, finance and decentralized finance (DeFi), blockchain and Web3 ecosystems, and other emerging sectors including supply chain management and content verification.

The significance of zkML applications extends beyond theoretical frameworks to real-world implementations that address fundamental challenges in modern digital systems. Recent developments have demonstrated that zkML is not merely an academic curiosity but a practical solution to pressing industry needs. As one leading practitioner noted, "zkML is 2024's answer to Silicon Valley's trust deficit, propelled by crypto giants like Polychain and a16z funneling millions into startups such as Modulus Labs, World (formerly Worldcoin), and Ingonyama to advance on-chain AI privacy and verifiability."[1]

5.1 Healthcare and Biomedical Applications

Healthcare represents one of the most compelling application domains for zkML, where the intersection of sensitive personal data, regulatory compliance requirements, and the need for verifiable AI-driven insights creates an ideal environment for zero-knowledge technologies. The healthcare sector faces unique challenges in deploying machine learning systems due to stringent privacy regulations such as HIPAA in the United States and GDPR in Europe, combined with the critical nature of medical decision-making that demands both accuracy and accountability.

Privacy-Preserving Diagnostics and Model Verification

The implementation of zkML in healthcare begins with privacy-preserving diagnostics, where medical institutions can leverage powerful AI models for disease detection and diagnosis without exposing sensitive patient data. Recent research has demonstrated that "healthcare data are sensitive; therefore, privacy is the first design principle in healthcare systems. With ZKML, healthcare providers can share insights derived from ML models without exposing the underlying patient data."[2] This capability addresses a fundamental challenge in medical AI, where the need for data sharing to improve model performance conflicts with patient privacy rights.

A practical example of this application involves medical imaging analysis, where hospitals can use zkML to prove that their AI systems correctly identified specific conditions in radiology scans without revealing the actual images or patient information. For instance, a hospital could demonstrate that their diagnostic AI achieved a 95% accuracy rate in detecting pneumonia from chest X-rays while keeping both the training data and the specific diagnostic details confidential. This approach enables medical institutions to validate their AI systems' performance for regulatory compliance and peer review without compromising patient confidentiality.

The technical implementation of privacy-preserving diagnostics involves converting neural network models used for medical image analysis into zero-knowledge circuits. Research published in PMC demonstrates that zkML frameworks can reduce model complexity specifically for healthcare applications while maintaining diagnostic accuracy.[3] This model complexity reduction becomes crucial when dealing with the computational overhead of generating zero-knowledge proofs for large neural networks typically used in medical imaging.

Federated Learning and Collaborative Research

Healthcare zkML applications extend beyond individual diagnostic systems to enable secure collaborative research across multiple institutions. Traditional federated learning approaches in healthcare face challenges related to data leakage and model inversion attacks, where adversaries can potentially reconstruct patient data from model updates. ZkML addresses these vulnerabilities by ensuring that collaborative learning occurs without exposing sensitive information even at the aggregation level.

A recent systematic review on privacy-preserving machine learning techniques in healthcare emphasizes that "to maintain ethical accountability and public trust, ML in healthcare must be executed with resilient Privacy-Preserving algorithms."[4] This requirement has led to the development of zkML systems that enable multiple hospitals to jointly train diagnostic models without sharing raw patient data. Each participating institution can contribute to model improvement while maintaining complete confidentiality of their patient populations.

The implementation involves each healthcare provider generating zero-knowledge proofs of their local model updates, which are then aggregated to improve the global model. This approach has shown particular promise in rare disease research, where no single institution has sufficient data to train effective models independently. By leveraging zkML, researchers can combine insights from multiple sources while ensuring that individual patient records remain completely private.

Regulatory Compliance and Audit Capabilities

Healthcare zkML applications also address the critical need for regulatory compliance and audit capabilities in medical AI systems. Regulatory bodies increasingly require transparency in AI-driven medical decisions, yet this transparency must be balanced against patient privacy rights. ZkML provides a sophisticated solution by enabling healthcare providers to demonstrate compliance with regulatory requirements without exposing sensitive data.

For example, the FDA's growing requirements for AI/ML-based medical devices include provisions for post-market surveillance and real-world evidence generation. As noted in recent research, "as of August 2024, the US FDA had authorized approximately 950 medical devices that use AI or machine learning."[5] ZkML enables manufacturers of these devices to provide verifiable evidence of their systems' performance in real-world settings without compromising patient privacy.

The audit capabilities extend to proving that medical AI systems operate within their intended scope and maintain consistent performance across different patient populations. Healthcare providers can generate zero-knowledge proofs demonstrating that their diagnostic systems maintain accuracy rates above specified thresholds without revealing the specific cases or patient characteristics that contributed to these measurements.

Challenges and Limitations in Healthcare zkML

Despite the promising applications, healthcare zkML faces several significant challenges. The computational overhead associated with generating zero-knowledge proofs for complex medical AI models remains substantial, often requiring specialized hardware and significant processing time. Current implementations show that "proving complex models (GPT-4o, etc.) remains prohibitively expensive, with hardware constraints limiting ROI niche use cases."[6]

Additionally, the quantization required to convert floating-point neural networks into integer-based zero-knowledge circuits can result in accuracy degradation. This challenge is particularly critical in healthcare applications where even small reductions in diagnostic accuracy can have significant clinical implications. Ongoing research focuses on developing more efficient proof systems and optimization techniques to minimize these accuracy losses while maintaining the privacy guarantees essential to healthcare applications.

5.2 Finance and DeFi Applications

The financial services sector represents another critical domain for zkML applications, where the intersection of sensitive financial data, regulatory requirements, and the need for verifiable algorithmic decision-making creates compelling use cases. Traditional financial systems rely heavily on machine learning for risk assessment, fraud detection, and algorithmic trading, but these applications often operate as black boxes that lack transparency and verifiability. ZkML addresses these limitations by enabling financial institutions to prove the correctness of their AI-driven decisions without revealing proprietary algorithms or sensitive customer data.

Verifiable Credit Scoring and Risk Assessment

Credit scoring represents one of the most promising applications of zkML in traditional finance. Current credit scoring systems suffer from opacity and potential bias, making it difficult for both consumers and regulators to understand how credit decisions are made. ZkML enables financial institutions to provide verifiable proof that their credit scoring algorithms operate fairly and accurately without revealing the specific factors or algorithms used in the assessment process.

A practical implementation involves financial institutions using zkML to prove that their credit scoring models meet specific fairness criteria across different demographic groups without exposing individual customer data or the proprietary scoring algorithms. For example, a bank could demonstrate that their lending algorithm maintains consistent approval rates across different geographic regions while keeping both the customer data and the specific algorithmic parameters confidential.

The technical implementation involves converting the bank's machine learning models for credit assessment into zero-knowledge circuits that can generate proofs of correct computation. Recent research indicates that "a decentralized lending platform uses zkML to evaluate a borrower's creditworthiness. The system generates a Zero-Knowledge Proof that verifies the borrower's credit score exceeds a required threshold without revealing their financial data or the model used."[7]

Fraud Detection and Anti-Money Laundering

Financial fraud detection represents another critical application area where zkML provides significant advantages over traditional approaches. Current fraud detection systems face the challenge of balancing accuracy with privacy, particularly when sharing information across financial institutions or with regulatory authorities. ZkML enables financial institutions to prove that their fraud detection systems correctly identified suspicious transactions without revealing the specific transaction details or the proprietary detection algorithms.

Recent industry developments show that "deepfake fraud incidents rose tenfold from 2022 to 2023, with 88% in the crypto sector."[8] This dramatic increase in sophisticated fraud attempts necessitates more advanced detection systems that can be verified without compromising the security of the detection methods themselves. ZkML provides a solution by enabling financial institutions to demonstrate the effectiveness of their fraud detection systems while maintaining the confidentiality necessary to prevent adversarial adaptation.

The application extends to anti-money laundering (AML) compliance, where financial institutions must demonstrate compliance with regulatory requirements while protecting customer privacy. ZkML enables banks to prove that their transaction monitoring systems correctly flagged suspicious activities according to regulatory criteria without revealing specific transaction patterns or customer information.

Decentralized Finance (DeFi) Applications

The DeFi sector has emerged as a particularly active area for zkML implementation, where the need for transparency and verifiability aligns with the privacy and security benefits provided by zero-knowledge technologies. DeFi protocols face unique challenges in implementing AI-driven decision-making while maintaining the decentralized and trustless nature of blockchain systems.

Recent analysis indicates that "in 2024 alone, over $1.8 billion was lost to exploits, rug pulls, and protocol vulnerabilities" in the DeFi space.[9] This has created urgent demand for verifiable AI systems that can detect and prevent various forms of financial manipulation without relying on centralized authorities. ZkML addresses this need by enabling DeFi protocols to implement sophisticated risk management and fraud detection systems that can be verified by the community.

Practical implementations include automated market makers (AMMs) that use zkML to prove they execute trades according to specified algorithms without front-running or other forms of manipulation. For example, a DeFi protocol could demonstrate that their yield optimization strategies perform as advertised by generating zero-knowledge proofs of their algorithmic decisions without revealing the specific trading strategies that could be exploited by arbitrageurs.

Trading Bot Verification and Algorithmic Transparency

Algorithmic trading represents a significant application area for zkML in both traditional finance and DeFi. Trading algorithms are typically proprietary and closely guarded secrets, yet there is increasing demand for transparency and verifiability, particularly in regulated markets and decentralized protocols.

ZkML enables the creation of verifiable trading bots that can prove their performance and compliance with specified trading rules without revealing their specific strategies. Modulus Labs has demonstrated this concept through their RockyBot project, which represents "the zero-knowledge secured fighting game where human players train AIs to battle one another. Zero-knowledge allows players to trust that their opponents have really trained the way they've said they have."[10]

The application extends to proving that trading algorithms operate within specified risk parameters and comply with regulatory requirements. For example, a high-frequency trading firm could use zkML to demonstrate to regulators that their algorithms do not engage in market manipulation while keeping their specific trading strategies confidential.

Regulatory Compliance and Reporting

Financial regulatory compliance represents a critical application area where zkML provides significant advantages over traditional approaches. Financial institutions face increasing regulatory requirements for transparency and accountability in their AI-driven decision-making processes, yet they must also protect proprietary algorithms and sensitive customer data.

ZkML enables financial institutions to provide verifiable proof of regulatory compliance without exposing the specific details of their compliance processes or customer data. For example, a bank could prove to regulators that their lending practices comply with fair lending laws across different demographic groups without revealing individual loan applications or the specific algorithms used in the lending process.

The approach has gained particular attention in the context of emerging digital asset regulations, where financial institutions must demonstrate compliance with new requirements while operating in rapidly evolving regulatory environments. Recent analysis suggests that "regulatory scrutiny has also affected user experiences, as platforms must balance accessibility with legal requirements."[11]

5.3 Blockchain and Web3 Applications

The blockchain and Web3 ecosystem represents perhaps the most natural application domain for zkML, where the intersection of decentralized systems, the need for verifiable computation, and privacy requirements creates compelling use cases. The transparent nature of blockchain systems often conflicts with privacy requirements, while the need for decentralized decision-making demands verifiable algorithmic processes. ZkML addresses these fundamental tensions by enabling privacy-preserving and verifiable AI applications within blockchain environments.

Solving the Oracle Problem with Verifiable AI

The oracle problem represents one of the most significant challenges in blockchain systems, where smart contracts require access to external data but must maintain trustless operation. Traditional oracle solutions introduce centralization risks and potential points of failure that compromise the decentralized nature of blockchain systems. ZkML provides a sophisticated solution by enabling the creation of verifiable AI-driven oracles that can process external data and provide authenticated results to smart contracts.

Recent developments in this area focus on creating "privacy-preserving cross-chain oracle" systems that leverage zero-knowledge technology.[12] The implementation involves AI models that process external data sources and generate zero-knowledge proofs of their computational correctness, which can then be verified by smart contracts without requiring trust in the oracle provider.

Practical applications include financial data feeds where AI models aggregate and analyze market data from multiple sources, generating verifiable price feeds for DeFi protocols. The zkML approach ensures that the price feeds are computed correctly while protecting the proprietary algorithms and data sources used in the aggregation process. This addresses a critical vulnerability in current DeFi systems where oracle manipulation has led to significant financial losses.

Biometric Verification and Digital Identity

Biometric verification represents one of the most prominent applications of zkML in the Web3 space, exemplified by Worldcoin's implementation of iris-based proof of personhood. The project demonstrates how zkML can enable large-scale biometric verification while maintaining privacy through zero-knowledge proofs.

Worldcoin's approach involves using specialized hardware (Orbs) to capture iris scans, which are then processed by AI models to generate unique identity proofs. The system leverages zkML to prove that each user is unique without storing or revealing the actual biometric data. As recent analysis notes, "Worldcoin utilizes zero-knowledge proofs (ZKPs) to enhance privacy and security within its World ID system. Worldcoin employs ZKPs to confirm a user's unique identity and humanity without disclosing any personal information."[13]

The technical implementation involves the Semaphore protocol, which enables users to prove membership in a group (verified humans) without revealing their specific identity. This approach has significant implications for Web3 applications that require proof of personhood, such as decentralized governance systems, fair token distributions, and Sybil-resistant voting mechanisms.

However, the approach has also faced significant challenges and criticism. Recent reports indicate that "a black market has emerged for the biometric information that is required for the project's verification process,"[14] highlighting the ongoing challenges in balancing accessibility with security in biometric systems.

Alternative Approaches to Digital Identity

The challenges faced by biometric-based systems have led to the development of alternative approaches to digital identity verification in Web3. Recent developments include non-biometric systems that leverage zero-knowledge proofs with government documents instead of biometric data.

Billions Network represents a notable example of this approach, securing "$30 million in funding from top-tier investors including Polychain Capital, Coinbase Ventures, Polygon Ventures, LCV, and Bitkraft Ventures to build the first universal human and AI verification network."[15] Their approach "uses zero-knowledge proofs with government documents instead of biometric iris scanning, providing global accessibility without specialized hardware requirements or invasive data collection."[16]

This alternative approach addresses several limitations of biometric systems, including regulatory concerns, accessibility challenges in regions without specialized hardware, and privacy concerns about biometric data collection. The system demonstrates how zkML can be applied to identity verification using readily available documents and standard mobile devices.

Decentralized Autonomous Organizations (DAOs) and Governance

ZkML applications in DAO governance represent an emerging area where the technology enables more sophisticated and verifiable decision-making processes. Traditional DAO governance systems often rely on simple token-weighted voting mechanisms that can be vulnerable to various forms of manipulation and fail to account for the complexity of organizational decision-making.

ZkML enables DAOs to implement sophisticated governance algorithms that can prove correct operation while maintaining the privacy of individual voting decisions and the confidentiality of proprietary governance strategies. For example, a DAO could implement reputation-based voting systems that weight member contributions based on verified past performance without revealing the specific algorithms or individual reputation scores.

Recent research indicates that zkML can enable "programmatically freeze hacked contracts using ZK-anomaly proofs, trained on historical exploit patterns."[17] This application demonstrates how DAOs can implement automated security responses based on AI analysis of transaction patterns while proving that their security systems operate correctly.

Smart Contract Intelligence and Automation

The integration of AI capabilities into smart contracts represents a fundamental expansion of blockchain functionality, yet traditional approaches face significant limitations due to the computational constraints and transparency requirements of blockchain systems. ZkML enables the creation of intelligent smart contracts that can make complex decisions based on AI analysis while maintaining verifiability and privacy.

Practical applications include automated market makers that adjust their parameters based on AI analysis of market conditions, lending protocols that dynamically adjust interest rates based on risk assessments, and insurance contracts that process claims automatically based on AI analysis of evidence. The zkML approach ensures that these systems can prove their correct operation while protecting proprietary algorithms and sensitive data.

Recent developments show that "smart contracts to be able to consume trusted inferences, verify their provenance, and have certainty in their quality."[18] This capability represents a significant advancement in smart contract functionality, enabling the development of more sophisticated decentralized applications that can respond intelligently to changing conditions.

5.4 Other Domains

Beyond healthcare, finance, and blockchain applications, zkML has demonstrated significant potential across a diverse range of other domains. These applications showcase the versatility of zero-knowledge machine learning and its ability to address privacy and verifiability challenges across various industries and use cases.

Supply Chain Management and Traceability

Supply chain management represents a critical application domain for zkML, where the need for transparency and traceability must be balanced against the protection of proprietary business information and trade secrets. Modern supply chains involve complex networks of suppliers, manufacturers, and distributors, each of whom may have sensitive information that should not be shared with competitors while still enabling verification of product authenticity and compliance.

ZkML enables supply chain participants to prove various aspects of their operations without revealing sensitive business information. For example, a manufacturer could prove that their products meet specific environmental standards without disclosing their supplier networks or detailed manufacturing processes. As recent analysis notes, "ZKPs can help verify the authenticity of products in a supply chain without revealing underlying trade secrets or confidential business information."[19]

The application extends to IoT-enabled supply chains where sensors monitor the condition and location of goods throughout the transportation process. ZkML enables the verification of sensor data and AI-driven analysis of product conditions without exposing sensitive logistics information or proprietary algorithms used for quality assessment.

Recent research demonstrates that "IoT devices transmit delicate information. Employing zero knowledge proof in cryptography, these devices may authenticate one another and exchange essential data without disclosing vulnerabilities."[20] This capability becomes particularly important in pharmaceutical supply chains where the integrity of temperature-sensitive medications must be verified without revealing specific transportation routes or storage facilities that could be vulnerable to security threats.

Content Verification and Deepfake Detection

The proliferation of AI-generated content, particularly deepfakes, has created urgent demand for reliable content verification systems. Traditional approaches to deepfake detection face the challenge of balancing accuracy with privacy, particularly when the detection algorithms themselves could be vulnerable to adversarial attacks if their specific operation is revealed.

ZkML provides a sophisticated solution by enabling content verification systems that can prove the authenticity or artificial nature of content without revealing the specific detection algorithms or the detailed analysis that led to the determination. This approach addresses several critical challenges in content verification, including the need to protect proprietary detection methods and the requirement to provide verifiable results that can be trusted by third parties.

Recent statistics indicate that "deepfake fraud incidents rose tenfold from 2022 to 2023,"[21] highlighting the urgent need for reliable detection systems. However, traditional detection approaches face the challenge that "the technology isn't sophisticated enough yet that people can't tell the generated videos aren't real, but the technology is improving rapidly."[22] This arms race between deepfake generation and detection technologies necessitates verification systems that can adapt quickly while maintaining verifiability.

The implementation of zkML in content verification involves training machine learning models to detect various forms of manipulated content and then converting these models into zero-knowledge circuits that can generate proofs of their analysis. Content platforms can then verify the authenticity of user-generated content while protecting both their detection algorithms and user privacy.

Gaming and Virtual Worlds

Gaming represents an emerging application domain for zkML where the technology enables new forms of provably fair gameplay and verifiable AI opponents. Traditional gaming systems often require players to trust that the game operates fairly and that AI opponents behave according to specified rules, but this trust requirement can be problematic in competitive gaming environments where significant value may be at stake.

ZkML enables the creation of provably fair gaming systems where players can verify that the game operates correctly without revealing the specific algorithms or random seeds that could be exploited. Modulus Labs has demonstrated this concept through their "Leela vs the World" project, described as "the first on-chain AI game where the community (The World) competes against an AI (Leela) in a game of chess."[23]

The application extends to virtual economies within gaming environments where AI-driven systems manage economic parameters and resource distribution. ZkML enables game operators to prove that their economic systems operate fairly while protecting the proprietary algorithms that prevent exploitation by sophisticated players.

Recent developments also explore the use of zkML in non-fungible token (NFT) systems where "zkML ensures fairness by validating game mechanics or NFT attributes based on external data or models without revealing proprietary information."[24] This capability enables the creation of dynamic NFTs whose attributes can be verified as correctly computed without revealing the specific algorithms used in their generation.

Academic Research and Scientific Computing

Academic research represents another important application domain for zkML, particularly in fields where research data is sensitive or where proprietary algorithms are used in scientific analysis. Traditional approaches to peer review and result verification in computational sciences face challenges when researchers cannot share their raw data or detailed methodologies due to privacy or intellectual property concerns.

ZkML enables researchers to provide verifiable proof of their computational results without revealing sensitive data or proprietary algorithms. This capability has particular importance in fields such as pharmaceutical research, where clinical trial data must remain confidential, or in social science research where participant privacy must be protected.

The implementation involves converting research algorithms into zero-knowledge circuits that can generate proofs of correct computation. Peer reviewers can then verify that the results were computed correctly according to the claimed methodology without accessing the raw data or the specific implementation details that might compromise intellectual property or participant privacy.

Energy and Environmental Monitoring

Environmental monitoring and energy management represent emerging application areas for zkML where the technology addresses the need for verifiable environmental compliance while protecting proprietary operational data. Energy companies and industrial facilities face increasing regulatory requirements for environmental monitoring and reporting, yet they must also protect competitive information about their operations.

ZkML enables organizations to prove compliance with environmental regulations without revealing detailed operational data that could compromise competitive positions. For example, a manufacturing facility could prove that their emissions remain within regulatory limits without revealing specific production processes or operational schedules that competitors could exploit.

The application extends to renewable energy systems where AI algorithms optimize energy production and distribution based on weather forecasts and demand patterns. ZkML enables energy providers to prove that their systems operate efficiently and fairly while protecting proprietary optimization algorithms and sensitive grid operation data.

Recent research on "zero-knowledge machine learning models for blockchain peer-to-peer energy trading"[25] demonstrates the potential for zkML to enable new forms of decentralized energy markets where participants can prove the authenticity and characteristics of their energy production without revealing sensitive operational information.

The diverse applications of zkML across these various domains demonstrate the technology's potential to address fundamental challenges in privacy-preserving computation and verifiable AI systems. As the technology continues to mature and computational efficiency improves, we can expect to see expanded adoption across an even broader range of applications, each leveraging the unique capabilities of zero-knowledge machine learning to balance transparency, privacy, and verifiability in ways that were previously impossible.

Footnotes:

[1] "What is zkML? Simple Explanation & Use Cases," DataWallet, January 28, 2025, https://www.datawallet.com/crypto/what-is-zkml.

[2] "Model Complexity Reduction for ZKML Healthcare Applications," PMC, 2024, https://pmc.ncbi.nlm.nih.gov/articles/PMC11624495/.

[3] Ibid.

[4] "Systematic review on privacy-preserving machine learning techniques for healthcare data," Journal of Cyber Security Technology, 2025, https://www.tandfonline.com/doi/full/10.1080/23742917.2025.2511145.

[5] "2025 Watch List: Artificial Intelligence in Health Care," NCBI Bookshelf, https://www.ncbi.nlm.nih.gov/books/NBK613808/.

[6] "What is zkML? Simple Explanation & Use Cases."

[7] "Zero-Knowledge Machine Learning (zkML)," CoinAPI Glossary, https://www.coinapi.io/learn/glossary/zkml.

[8] "2024 Deepfakes Guide and Statistics," Security.org, August 26, 2025, https://www.security.org/resources/deepfake-statistics/.

[9] "AI-Powered Fraud Detection in DeFi," Smart Liquidity Research, May 21, 2025, https://smartliquidity.info/2025/05/21/ai-powered-fraud-detection-in-defi/.

[10] "The State of Zero-Knowledge Machine Learning (zkML)," Spectral Finance, March 25, 2024, https://blog.spectral.finance/the-state-of-zero-knowledge-machine-learning-zkml/.

[11] "Risk Management in DeFi," MDPI, January 16, 2025, https://www.mdpi.com/1911-8074/18/1/38.

[12] "ZK Oracle: the Community-driven & Privacy-preserving Cross-chain Oracle for Web3," ZKOracle Medium, December 16, 2021, https://medium.com/zkoracle/zk-oracle-the-privacy-preserving-cross-chain-oracle-for-web3-7bdca013fa0b.

[13] "Top Zero-Knowledge (ZK) Proof Crypto Projects of 2025," KuCoin Learn, https://www.kucoin.com/learn/crypto/top-zero-knowledge-zk-proof-crypto-projects.

[14] "Worldcoin faces privacy concerns as iris scan black market emerges," CryptoSlate, March 6, 2024, https://cryptoslate.com/worldcoin-biometric-verification-faces-privacy-concerns-as-black-market-for-iris-scans-emerges/.

[15] "Billions Network Review: $30M Non-Biometric ID Platform 2025," Jucoin Blog, August 1, 2025, https://blog.jucoin.com/billions-network-review/.

[16] Ibid.

[17] "What is zkML? Simple Explanation & Use Cases."

[18] "Spectral on LinkedIn: The State of Zero-Knowledge Machine Learning (zkML)," LinkedIn, June 6, 2023, https://www.linkedin.com/posts/spectralfinance_the-state-of-zero-knowledge-machine-learning-activity-7071936963255169025-2pvZ.

[19] "Top Zero-Knowledge (ZK) Proof Crypto Projects of 2025."

[20] "Exploring Blockchain with Zero Knowledge Proof Uses," Debut Infotech, https://www.debutinfotech.com/blog/zero-knowledge-proof-uses.

[21] "2024 Deepfakes Guide and Statistics."

[22] "Improved Technology for Deepfakes Highlights a Supply Chain Problem," IEEE Spectrum, March 29, 2023, https://spectrum.ieee.org/deepfakes-supply-chain.

[23] "Exploring Modulus Labs & ZK-ML," Darshan Gandhi, August 29, 2023, https://darshang.substack.com/p/exploring-modulus-labs-and-zk-ml.

[24] "Zero-Knowledge Machine Learning (zkML)."

[25] "Zero-knowledge machine learning models for blockchain peer-to-peer energy trading," Internet of Things and the Environment, 2025, https://www.sciencedirect.com/science/article/pii/S2542660525001520.

Chapter 6: Challenges and Limitations of Zero-Knowledge Machine Learning

Despite the transformative potential of zero-knowledge machine learning (zkML), significant challenges continue to impede its widespread adoption and practical implementation. These obstacles span technical, operational, security, and regulatory dimensions, each presenting unique barriers that must be addressed for zkML to achieve its full potential. This chapter provides a comprehensive examination of these challenges, offering a balanced perspective that acknowledges both current limitations and potential mitigation strategies.

6.1 Computational and Efficiency Issues

6.1.1 Proof Generation Overhead

The most significant barrier to zkML adoption remains the substantial computational overhead associated with generating zero-knowledge proofs. Current systems demonstrate proving times that are orders of magnitude higher than standard ML inference, creating practical limitations for real-world deployment.

Recent benchmarking reveals the severity of this challenge. For instance, generating a zero-knowledge proof for GPT-2 inference requires approximately 3 hours on high-end hardware, with some implementations demanding even more substantial resources[1]. The Modulus Labs implementation of zkLLM, when proving GPT-2 XL (a model with approximately 1 billion parameters), required a 128-core CPU, 1TB of RAM, and over 200 hours for a single proof generation[2]. This represents a computational overhead that is several thousand times greater than the original inference computation.

Contemporary zkML frameworks have made significant strides in addressing these efficiency concerns. The ZKML system developed by Chen et al. demonstrates remarkable improvements, achieving up to 5× faster proving times compared to earlier zk-SNARK systems while maintaining verification speeds up to 22× faster than existing methods[3]. Additionally, proof sizes have been compressed by up to 22×, significantly reducing storage and bandwidth requirements. These optimizations stem from adaptive layer implementations that select optimal "gadgets" for each neural network layer and dynamic hardware adaptability that tailors circuit designs to specific hardware constraints.

However, even with these improvements, the computational requirements remain prohibitive for many applications. The fundamental challenge lies in the mathematical complexity of converting neural network operations into arithmetic circuits suitable for zero-knowledge proof systems. Each multiplication, addition, and non-linear activation function must be expressed as constraints within the proof system, leading to circuit sizes that grow exponentially with model complexity.

6.1.2 Scalability Limitations with Large Models

The scalability challenge becomes particularly acute when considering state-of-the-art large language models (LLMs) and modern deep learning architectures. While zkML frameworks have successfully demonstrated proofs for models like GPT-2 and various vision models, scaling to contemporary LLMs with hundreds of billions of parameters remains largely infeasible[4].

Vitalik Buterin has highlighted this fundamental limitation, noting that implementing models like GPT-4 or Claude 3 Opus using zk-SNARKs is practically impossible with current technology[5]. The computational resources required would be exponentially larger than those already substantial requirements for smaller models. This scalability gap represents a critical barrier to zkML adoption in applications requiring cutting-edge AI capabilities.

Current cryptographic primitives lack the performance necessary to handle very large model architectures efficiently[6]. The computational overhead of proving systems makes them impractical for state-of-the-art models with billions of parameters, creating a significant gap between what zkML can verify and what modern AI applications require.

6.1.3 Hardware and Memory Constraints

The hardware requirements for zkML proof generation present additional practical challenges. Proof generation is typically limited by memory capacity rather than computational speed, with memory requirements scaling rapidly as model size increases[7]. This creates bottlenecks that cannot be easily resolved through traditional hardware acceleration approaches.

RAM consumption and proof generation time scale quickly as model size grows, necessitating specialized hardware configurations that may not be readily available or cost-effective for many applications[8]. The reliance on high-end GPUs and substantial memory configurations introduces centralization risks, as only organizations with significant computational resources can feasibly generate proofs for moderately complex models.

Several proving systems have emerged to address these challenges, including GKR-based systems that use sumcheck protocols and layered arithmetic circuits, as well as compositional techniques that combine efficient proving systems like Plonky2 with proof compression methods like Groth16[9]. However, managing the tradeoffs between proving time, memory requirements, and proof size remains a core challenge for projects building zkML applications.

6.2 Technical Hurdles

6.2.1 Parameter Distortion and Quantization Challenges

The conversion of machine learning models into zero-knowledge proof circuits introduces inevitable parameter distortion that can significantly impact model accuracy. This distortion occurs through multiple mechanisms during the zkML workflow, from initial model conversion to circuit optimization for proof generation.

Quantization represents one of the primary sources of parameter distortion in zkML systems. To make models compatible with arithmetic circuits, floating-point weights must be converted to fixed-point representations, introducing quantization errors that can accumulate throughout the network[10]. Research in model compression demonstrates that even carefully designed quantization schemes can result in significant accuracy degradation, particularly at lower bit-widths[11].

The challenge is compounded by the fact that different layers of neural networks exhibit varying sensitivity to quantization. While some layers may tolerate aggressive quantization with minimal accuracy loss, others require higher precision to maintain acceptable performance[12]. This necessitates sophisticated mixed-precision quantization strategies that balance circuit complexity with model accuracy.

Furthermore, the constraint systems used in zero-knowledge proofs impose additional limitations on numerical precision. Finite field arithmetic, which forms the foundation of most zk-SNARK systems, operates with different numerical properties than standard floating-point arithmetic, potentially introducing subtle but significant changes to model behavior[13].

6.2.2 Non-Linear Activation Function Handling

Neural networks rely heavily on non-linear activation functions such as ReLU, sigmoid, and tanh to capture complex patterns in data. However, these non-linearities pose significant challenges for zkML implementations, as they are difficult to express efficiently within arithmetic circuits[14].

The fundamental issue stems from the mathematical operations supported by zero-knowledge proof systems. While linear operations like matrix multiplications and additions can be naturally expressed as arithmetic constraints, non-linear functions require more complex circuit constructions that dramatically increase proof generation time and circuit size.

Modern zkML frameworks have developed several approaches to address this challenge. Plonkish proof systems, including Halo2 and Plonky2, utilize custom gates and lookup tables to implement non-linearities more efficiently[15]. These systems precompute the possible outcomes of non-linear functions and store them in lookup tables, which proves to be computationally more efficient than direct circuit implementation.

However, these solutions come with their own limitations. Lookup tables require significant memory overhead and may not support the full range of activation functions used in modern neural networks. Additionally, the approximation errors introduced by discretized lookup tables can accumulate across network layers, potentially impacting overall model performance.

6.2.3 Integration Complexity with Existing ML Frameworks

The integration of zkML capabilities with existing machine learning development workflows presents substantial technical challenges. Most zkML systems require significant modifications to standard ML pipelines, from model training to deployment, creating barriers to adoption for practitioners familiar with conventional frameworks.

Current zkML toolchains often require models to be exported to specialized formats (such as ONNX) and then converted to circuit representations using domain-specific languages like Circom[16]. This conversion process is neither straightforward nor automated, requiring deep expertise in both machine learning and cryptographic proof systems.

The lack of standardized interfaces between ML frameworks and zkML tools creates additional friction. Developers must navigate multiple toolchains, each with its own syntax, optimization strategies, and limitations. This complexity is exacerbated by the rapid evolution of both ML frameworks and zkML tools, making it difficult to maintain stable integration pipelines.

Moreover, the debugging and optimization processes for zkML systems differ fundamentally from traditional ML workflows. Identifying performance bottlenecks, accuracy degradation sources, and circuit optimization opportunities requires specialized knowledge that extends beyond conventional ML expertise.

6.2.4 Model Architecture Limitations

Not all neural network architectures are equally suitable for zkML implementation. The complexity of converting different architectural components to arithmetic circuits varies significantly, with some modern architectures presenting nearly insurmountable challenges for current zkML systems.

Attention mechanisms, which form the core of transformer architectures, involve complex operations like softmax normalization and multi-head attention computations that are expensive to implement in zero-knowledge proofs[17]. While recent work has demonstrated zkML implementations for models like GPT-2, scaling to modern transformer architectures with hundreds of layers and attention heads remains challenging.

Similarly, advanced architectural components like batch normalization, dropout, and sophisticated regularization techniques may not have direct equivalents in zkML circuits, requiring either approximation or elimination during the conversion process. These modifications can impact model performance and may necessitate retraining or fine-tuning specifically for zkML compatibility.

6.3 Security and Distributed Systems Challenges

6.3.1 Vulnerabilities in Zero-Knowledge Proof Systems

While zero-knowledge proofs provide strong theoretical security guarantees, practical implementations face various vulnerabilities that can compromise the entire zkML system. The security of zkML systems depends not only on the underlying cryptographic protocols but also on the correct implementation of complex proving systems.

Recent security audits have revealed significant vulnerabilities in production zkML systems. For instance, the Polygon zkEVM audit identified 10 critical, 1 high, and 4 medium-level vulnerabilities within the prover component that generates proofs for valid state transitions[18]. These vulnerabilities highlight the gap between theoretical security and practical implementation security.

The complexity of ZK proof systems creates multiple attack vectors. Implementation bugs, particularly in circuit compilation and proof generation, can lead to situations where invalid computations are accepted as valid proofs[19].

Such vulnerabilities are particularly concerning in zkML applications where the correctness of AI model outputs is critical for application security.

Furthermore, side-channel attacks represent an emerging threat to zkML systems. The computational patterns during proof generation may leak information about the underlying model or input data, potentially undermining the privacy guarantees that zkML aims to provide[20].

6.3.2 Adversarial Attacks on Neural Networks in zkML Context

Neural networks are susceptible to various adversarial attacks that can manipulate model outputs, and these vulnerabilities extend to zkML implementations with additional complexity. The zero-knowledge nature of zkML systems can potentially obscure adversarial manipulations, making detection more challenging.

Common adversarial attack vectors include Gaussian noise injection, data poisoning during training, and membership inference attacks (MIAs) that can reveal whether specific data was used in model training[21]. In the zkML context, these attacks are particularly problematic because the privacy-preserving nature of the system can mask the detection of such manipulations.

Membership inference attacks pose a specific threat to zkML systems that are designed to maintain training data privacy. If an attacker can determine whether specific data points were included in the training set, this directly contradicts the privacy guarantees that zkML aims to provide[22].

The verification process in zkML systems focuses on computational correctness rather than adversarial robustness, creating potential blind spots where maliciously crafted inputs could pass verification while producing incorrect or manipulated outputs.

6.3.3 Economic and Incentive Alignment Issues

Decentralized zkML systems face complex economic challenges related to incentive alignment and cost distribution. The high computational cost of proof generation creates economic barriers that may centralize power among actors with significant resources, contradicting the decentralization goals of many zkML applications.

The disparity between proof generation costs and verification costs creates asymmetric economic incentives. While verification is fast and inexpensive, proof generation requires substantial computational resources, potentially creating monopolistic dynamics where only well-resourced actors can participate as provers[23].

This economic asymmetry raises concerns about the long-term sustainability of decentralized zkML networks. If proof generation becomes economically viable only for a small number of actors, the resulting centralization could undermine the trust and transparency benefits that zkML aims to provide.

6.3.4 Third-Party Dependency Risks

Many zkML implementations rely on third-party services, libraries, and infrastructure components that introduce additional security and reliability risks. These dependencies can range from cloud computing services for proof generation to specialized cryptographic libraries for circuit implementation.

Third-party AI APIs and models used in zkML systems may harbor unseen vulnerabilities or non-compliance with regulatory standards[24]. The algorithms and data used by external partners may contain hidden biases, backdoors, or other malicious elements that remain undetected until exploited.

The complexity of the zkML technology stack increases the attack surface, as vulnerabilities in any component can potentially compromise the entire system. This includes dependencies on specific versions of cryptographic libraries, proving systems, and circuit compilation tools.

6.4 Ethical and Regulatory Considerations

6.4.1 Privacy vs. Accountability Tension

One of the fundamental ethical challenges in zkML lies in balancing privacy preservation with accountability and auditability requirements. While zkML enables verification of computations without revealing sensitive data, this same privacy can potentially obscure important information needed for ethical oversight and regulatory compliance.

The "black box" nature of zkML systems can make it difficult to assess whether AI models exhibit bias, discrimination, or other ethical concerns[25]. Traditional approaches to AI fairness and bias detection often require access to model internals, training data, or decision-making processes that zkML deliberately conceals.

This tension is particularly acute in high-stakes applications such as healthcare, criminal justice, and financial services, where both privacy and accountability are essential. Regulatory bodies may require explainability and auditability that conflicts with the privacy guarantees of zkML systems.

The challenge extends to incident response and debugging scenarios. When zkML systems produce unexpected or problematic outputs, investigating the root cause may require access to information that the zero-knowledge properties are designed to protect.

6.4.2 Regulatory Compliance Complexity

The regulatory landscape for AI systems is rapidly evolving, with new frameworks and requirements emerging across multiple jurisdictions. zkML systems must navigate this complex and changing regulatory environment while maintaining their privacy-preserving properties.

The European Union's Artificial Intelligence Act, expected to take full effect by 2026, introduces risk-based regulations that categorize AI systems based on their potential impact[26]. High-risk AI applications in areas like law enforcement and employment will be subject to strict compliance standards that may conflict with zkML's privacy-preserving approach.

Similarly, sector-specific regulations in healthcare (HIPAA), finance (GDPR, SOX), and other industries impose transparency and auditability requirements that may be challenging to satisfy with current zkML implementations. The need to prove compliance with these regulations while maintaining zero-knowledge properties represents a significant technical and legal challenge.

The global nature of many AI applications further complicates compliance, as zkML systems may need to simultaneously satisfy different regulatory requirements across multiple jurisdictions with potentially conflicting privacy and transparency mandates.

6.4.3 Standardization and Interoperability Challenges

The lack of standardized frameworks, protocols, and best practices for zkML implementations creates significant barriers to adoption and poses risks for long-term sustainability. Without clear standards, different zkML systems may be incompatible, limiting their utility and creating vendor lock-in scenarios.

The absence of standardized security evaluation criteria makes it difficult to assess and compare the security properties of different zkML implementations. This uncertainty can discourage adoption, particularly in risk-sensitive applications where security guarantees are paramount[27].

Interoperability challenges extend to integration with existing AI governance frameworks and compliance systems. Organizations need clear guidance on how zkML implementations fit within established risk management and governance structures.

6.4.4 Ethical AI Governance in zkML Context

Traditional AI ethics frameworks emphasize principles such as transparency, explainability, and fairness[28]. However, these principles may conflict with the privacy-preserving goals of zkML, necessitating new approaches to ethical AI governance.

The UNESCO AI Ethics Recommendation and similar frameworks emphasize the importance of human oversight, transparency, and accountability[29]. Adapting these principles to zkML systems requires careful consideration of how to maintain ethical oversight while preserving privacy guarantees.

The challenge is particularly complex in applications involving vulnerable populations or high-stakes decisions. Ensuring that zkML systems do not perpetuate or amplify bias requires new methodologies for fairness assessment that operate within zero-knowledge constraints.

Furthermore, the global nature of AI development and deployment means that zkML systems must navigate diverse ethical frameworks and cultural values across different societies and legal systems.

6.4.5 Professional and Educational Challenges

The specialized knowledge required for zkML development and deployment creates significant human resource challenges. The intersection of cryptography, machine learning, and distributed systems requires expertise that is rare and difficult to develop through traditional educational pathways.

Organizations seeking to implement zkML systems face talent shortages and must invest significantly in training and education[30]. This barrier to entry may limit zkML adoption to well-resourced organizations, potentially exacerbating existing inequalities in AI capabilities.

The rapid evolution of zkML technology also creates challenges for maintaining expertise and keeping pace with best practices. The field requires continuous learning and adaptation that may be difficult to sustain across diverse organizational contexts.

Mitigation Strategies and Future Directions

Despite these significant challenges, active research and development efforts are addressing many of the limitations identified in this chapter. Hardware acceleration initiatives, including specialized zkML processors and optimized proving systems, show promise for reducing computational overhead[31].

Advances in proof system efficiency, particularly through improved lookup arguments and custom gate designs, continue to narrow the performance gap between zkML and traditional ML systems. Compositional proving techniques and hybrid approaches that combine different proof systems offer additional pathways for optimization.

On the regulatory front, proactive engagement between the zkML community and regulatory bodies is essential for developing frameworks that balance privacy with accountability requirements. Industry standards organizations are beginning to address zkML-specific guidelines and best practices.

Educational initiatives and open-source development efforts are helping to build the expertise needed for widespread zkML adoption. Collaborative platforms and shared tooling can reduce the barriers to entry and accelerate innovation across the field.

Conclusion

The challenges and limitations examined in this chapter represent significant but not insurmountable barriers to zkML adoption. While computational overhead, technical complexity, security vulnerabilities, and regulatory uncertainty pose substantial obstacles, ongoing research and development efforts continue to address these issues systematically.

The path forward requires coordinated efforts across multiple domains: advancing cryptographic efficiency, developing robust security practices, establishing clear regulatory frameworks, and building educational capacity. Success in addressing these challenges will determine whether zkML can fulfill its promise of enabling privacy-preserving, verifiable artificial intelligence at scale.

Understanding these limitations is crucial for setting realistic expectations and making informed decisions about zkML implementation. As the field continues to mature, many of these challenges may be resolved through technological advancement and improved practices, but acknowledging and addressing them remains essential for responsible development and deployment of zkML systems.

Footnotes:

[1] Daniel Kang et al., "ZKML: An Optimizing System for ML Inference in Zero-Knowledge Proofs," *Proceedings of the Nineteenth European Conference on Computer Systems* (2024), accessed January 15, 2025, https://dl.acm.org/doi/10.1145/3627703.3650088.

[2] Gaudiy Lab, "Potential and Challenges of zkML. Is AI a Silver Bullet?" *Gaudiy Web3 and AI Lab*, November 24, 2024, accessed January 15, 2025, https://medium.com/gaudiy-web3-and-ai-lab/88022a0033a5.

[3] Zkrypto Inc., "ZKML: An Optimizing System for ML Inference in Zero-Knowledge Proofs," *Medium*, November 23, 2024, accessed January 15, 2025, https://zkrypto.medium.com/zkml-an-optimizing-system-for-ml-inference-in-zero-knowledge-proofs-f9e4cafbefbe.

[4] Kudelski Security, "ZKML: Verifiable Machine Learning using Zero-Knowledge Proof," *Modern CISO Blog*, April 8, 2025, accessed January 15, 2025, https://kudelskisecurity.com/modern-ciso-blog/zkml-verifiable-machine-learning-using-zero-knowledge-proof/.

[5] Gaudiy Lab, "Potential and Challenges of zkML."

[6] Kudelski Security, "ZKML: Verifiable Machine Learning using Zero-Knowledge Proof."

[7] Justin McAfee, "zkML: Evolving the Intelligence of Smart Contracts Through Zero-Knowledge Cryptography," *1kxnetwork*, February 17, 2024, accessed January 15, 2025, https://medium.com/1kxnetwork/zkml-evolving-the-intelligence-of-smart-contracts-through-zero-knowledge-cryptography-e6725412bbd1.

[8] Ibid.

[9] Ibid.

[10] A comprehensive overview of quantization challenges can be found in: HuangOwen, "Awesome LLM compression research papers and tools," *GitHub*, accessed January 15, 2025, https://github.com/HuangOwen/Awesome-LLM-Compression.

[11] Multiple studies on quantization accuracy loss are compiled in: Efficient-ML, "Awesome Model Quantization," *GitHub*, accessed January 15, 2025, https://github.com/Efficient-ML/Awesome-Model-Quantization.

[12] Rate-distortion analysis for model compression demonstrates varying layer sensitivity: Yang You et al., "Rate Distortion For Model Compression: From Theory To Practice," *arXiv preprint arXiv:1810.06401* (2024), accessed January 15, 2025, https://ar5iv.labs.arxiv.org/html/1810.06401.

[13] Technical details on finite field arithmetic limitations are discussed in various zkML implementation papers referenced throughout this work.

[14] McAfee, "zkML: Evolving the Intelligence of Smart Contracts."

[15] Ibid.

[16] Worldcoin, "An introduction to zero-knowledge machine learning (ZKML)," *Worldcoin Blog*, December 20, 2023, accessed January 15, 2025, https://world.org/blog/engineering/intro-to-zkml.

[17] Recent work on transformer implementations in zkML is referenced in survey papers on zkML applications.

[18] ZKV, "Security Vulnerabilities in ZK," May 20, 2024, accessed January 15, 2025, https://zkv.xyz/security-vulnerabilities-in-zk/.

[19] Ibid.

[20] Side-channel attacks on cryptographic systems are well-documented in the security literature and extend to ZK implementations.

[21] Kudelski Security, "ZKML: Verifiable Machine Learning using Zero-Knowledge Proof."

[22] Ibid.

[23] Economic challenges in decentralized systems are discussed in: DataWallet, "What is zkML? Simple Explanation & Use Cases," January 28, 2025, accessed January 15, 2025, https://www.datawallet.com/crypto/what-is-zkml.

[24] Kudelski Security, "ZKML: Verifiable Machine Learning using Zero-Knowledge Proof."

[25] Privacy vs. accountability tensions are fundamental to AI governance as discussed in: IBM, "What is AI Governance?" *IBM Think*, July 29, 2025, accessed January 15, 2025, https://www.ibm.com/think/topics/ai-governance.

[26] NAVEX, "Artificial Intelligence and Compliance: Preparing for the Future of AI Governance, Risk, and Compliance," February 13, 2025, accessed January 15, 2025, https://www.navex.com/en-us/blog/article/artificial-intelligence-and-compliance-preparing-for-the-future-of-ai-governance-risk-and-compliance/.

[27] Standardization challenges are discussed across multiple regulatory frameworks referenced in this chapter.

[28] European Commission, "Ethics guidelines for trustworthy AI," *Shaping Europe's digital future*, accessed January 15, 2025, https://digital-strategy.ec.europa.eu/en/library/ethics-guidelines-trustworthy-ai.

[29] UNESCO, "Ethics of Artificial Intelligence," September 26, 2024, accessed January 15, 2025, https://www.unesco.org/en/artificial-intelligence/recommendation-ethics.

[30] Talent shortage challenges are highlighted in: DataWallet, "What is zkML? Simple Explanation & Use Cases."

[31] Hardware acceleration efforts are mentioned in various industry reports and technical papers referenced throughout this work.

Chapter 7: Case Studies and Real-World Examples

The theoretical promise of zero-knowledge machine learning finds its true validation in real-world implementations. This chapter examines comprehensive case studies that demonstrate zkML's practical applications across diverse sectors, from biometric identity verification to decentralized finance, academic research, and emerging blockchain platforms. Through detailed analysis of implementation outcomes, technical challenges, and lessons learned, we explore how organizations are successfully integrating zkML into production systems while addressing privacy, scalability, and trust concerns.

7.1 Worldcoin and Biometric zkML: Proving Uniqueness Without Data Storage

The Vision of Universal Basic Identity

Worldcoin, co-founded by OpenAI CEO Sam Altman, represents one of the most ambitious implementations of zkML technology in the realm of biometric identity verification. The project aims to create a global "proof of personhood" system that can distinguish humans from artificial intelligence at scale, addressing what many consider to be one of the most pressing challenges in an age of increasingly sophisticated AI.[1]

The core innovation of Worldcoin lies in its integration of iris biometric scanning with zero-knowledge proofs to create World ID, a privacy-preserving digital identity protocol. Unlike traditional biometric systems that store sensitive biometric data in centralized databases, Worldcoin's approach fundamentally reimagines how biometric verification can operate while maintaining user privacy and preventing identity fraud.[2]

Technical Architecture and Implementation

The Orb: Custom Hardware for Trust

At the heart of Worldcoin's system is a sophisticated device called the Orb, a helmet-shaped biometric scanner specifically designed for iris recognition. The Orb incorporates multiple sensors beyond the primary iris camera, including:

- Wide-angle cameras for user positioning and steering the telephoto iris camera
- Near-infrared wide-angle cameras for enhanced imaging
- 3D time-of-flight cameras for depth perception and anti-spoofing
- Thermal cameras for additional fraud prevention measures[3]

This multi-sensor approach addresses the high incentive for fraud inherent in Worldcoin's model, where each person receives free cryptocurrency tokens upon verification. The system was designed from first principles, considering which measurable features distinguish genuine humans from spoofing attempts.[4]

Zero-Knowledge Proof Integration

The zkML implementation in Worldcoin operates through several key stages:

Biometric Capture and Processing: When a user approaches an Orb, their iris is scanned and the image is immediately processed using proprietary machine learning models. These models convert the raw iris image into a unique cryptographic identifier known as an iris code.[5]

Zero-Knowledge Proof Generation: Rather than storing the original biometric data or even the processed iris code, the system generates zero-knowledge proofs that demonstrate the uniqueness of the biometric without revealing any underlying biometric information. This process ensures mathematical impossibility of linking usage across applications.[6]

Semaphore Protocol Integration: Worldcoin utilizes the Semaphore protocol, a privacy gadget built on Ethereum, to enable anonymous signaling. Users can prove membership in the Worldcoin group and signal anonymously without revealing their specific identity, creating a robust framework for privacy-preserving verification.[7]

Implementation Challenges and Outcomes

Global Deployment and Scale

Since its official launch in July 2023, Worldcoin has achieved remarkable scale, with the collection of iris scans from over 4.5 million people across 120 countries.[8] This rapid expansion has provided valuable insights into the practical challenges of deploying zkML at global scale.

Regulatory Compliance: The project has faced significant regulatory scrutiny, particularly in Europe. Portugal's Data Protection Authority temporarily suspended Worldcoin's activities after the collection of iris scans from approximately 300,000 people, including minors.[9] This regulatory response highlighted the tension between innovative privacy-preserving technologies and existing data protection frameworks.

Technical Performance: Performance metrics demonstrate the practical viability of zkML for biometric verification. The system processes iris scans in real-time, generating zero-knowledge proofs that can be verified on-chain efficiently. The mathematical guarantees provided by the zero-knowledge proofs ensure that even Worldcoin itself cannot link users' World ID usage across different applications.[10]

Privacy and Security Outcomes

Data Minimization: One of the most significant achievements of Worldcoin's implementation is its demonstration of practical data minimization. The original iris scan is deleted immediately after processing, with only the zero-knowledge proof retained for verification purposes. This approach goes beyond regulatory requirements, implementing privacy-by-design principles.[11]

Cryptographic Assurances: The use of zero-knowledge proofs provides mathematical guarantees that traditional biometric systems cannot offer. Independent security audits have validated both the cryptographic protocols and smart contract implementations, providing confidence in the system's security properties.[12]

Expanding Applications and Future Development

Mobile Verification Research: Worldcoin is investigating zkML implementation on mobile devices for face authentication. This research aims to extend the secure hardware guarantees from the Orb to users' personal devices, though the team acknowledges that mobile implementations cannot provide the same security level as custom hardware.[13]

Integration Ecosystem: World ID 2.0, launched in December 2023, demonstrates practical integration with major platforms including Telegram, Reddit, Shopify, and Minecraft for passwordless authentication. This integration showcases how zkML-based identity systems can enhance existing applications without compromising user privacy.[14]

Lessons Learned and Industry Impact

Technical Insights

The Worldcoin implementation provides several critical insights for zkML deployment:

Hardware Requirements: The necessity of custom hardware for high-security biometric verification underscores the current limitations of software-only zkML solutions for certain applications. The Orb's sophisticated sensor array demonstrates that practical zkML often requires purpose-built infrastructure.

Scalability Considerations: Processing over 4.5 million users has revealed both the potential and limitations of current zkML technology. While the system can handle significant user volumes, the computational requirements for proof generation remain substantial.

User Experience Balance: Worldcoin's experience demonstrates the challenge of balancing security, privacy, and user experience. The requirement for physical presence at an Orb location creates friction but enables higher security guarantees.

Regulatory and Social Implications

Privacy Paradox: Despite providing stronger privacy protections than traditional biometric systems, Worldcoin has faced more regulatory scrutiny than conventional biometric implementations. This paradox highlights the need for better education about zkML's privacy advantages.

Global Digital Identity: The project has sparked important discussions about the feasibility and desirability of global digital identity systems, demonstrating both the technical possibilities and social challenges of such initiatives.

Future Trajectory and Acquisition

In December 2024, Tools for Humanity, the company behind Worldcoin, acquired Modulus Labs to enhance their zero-knowledge AI and cryptography research capabilities.[15] This acquisition signals continued investment in advancing zkML technology and suggests potential expansion of zkML applications beyond biometric verification.

The Worldcoin case study demonstrates that zkML can operate at significant scale while providing meaningful privacy protections. However, it also reveals the complexities of deploying such systems in diverse regulatory environments and the ongoing need for infrastructure investment to support zkML applications.

7.2 DeFi Platforms with zkML: NetworkNoya's AI-Powered Yield Optimization

Addressing DeFi's Complexity Challenge

The decentralized finance (DeFi) ecosystem has evolved into a complex, multi-chain landscape where yield opportunities are scattered across dozens of protocols and multiple blockchains. For most users, identifying optimal yield strategies while managing risk across this fragmented ecosystem has become nearly impossible. NetworkNoya emerges as a pioneering solution that leverages zero-knowledge machine learning to automate yield farming across multiple chains while maintaining trustless operation.[16]

Technical Architecture and Innovation

Zero-Knowledge Machine Learning Implementation

NetworkNoya's core innovation lies in its implementation of Zero-Knowledge Machine Learning (zkML) for trustless AI execution in DeFi. Traditional AI-powered DeFi platforms require users to trust that AI agents will act in their best interests. NetworkNoya's zkML implementation provides cryptographic proof that AI decisions are executed according to predefined parameters and user constraints, creating a trustless environment where users can benefit from sophisticated AI strategies without surrendering control over their funds.[17]

The platform's zkML system operates through several key components:

Predictive AI Models: NetworkNoya employs machine learning models that analyze on-chain and off-chain data to predict yields, assess risks, and optimize capital allocation across different protocols and chains. These models incorporate multiple data sources including:

- Historical yield performance across protocols
- Liquidity depth and volatility metrics
- Bridge fees and slippage analysis
- Market sentiment indicators
- Protocol security assessments[18]

Zero-Knowledge Proof Generation: Rather than requiring users to trust the AI's decision-making process, NetworkNoya generates zero-knowledge proofs that demonstrate the AI model has executed correctly according to its specified parameters. This approach ensures users can verify that their funds are being managed according to the agreed-upon strategy without revealing the proprietary model weights or sensitive trading data.[19]

Smart Liquidity System: The platform introduces a concept called "Smart Liquidity," which combines AI-driven decision making with zkML verification. This system ensures that liquidity movements only occur after cryptographic proof that the model has operated correctly, eliminating the trust assumptions typically placed on strategy managers.[20]

Omnichain Architecture

NetworkNoya's omnichain functionality addresses one of DeFi's most significant pain points: the need to manually bridge assets between different blockchains to capture yield opportunities. The platform's architecture includes:

Intelligent Bridge Aggregation: The system works with bridge and DEX aggregators to transfer and exchange assets across chains automatically. By analyzing real-time data about bridge fees, security, and speed, the AI models can optimize routing decisions while the zkML system provides proof of correct execution.[21]

Cross-Chain Risk Assessment: The platform's AI models assess risks across different chains, including:

- Smart contract security scores
- Bridge security and historical performance
- Chain-specific risks and governance issues
- Liquidity depth and market conditions

Automated Rebalancing: When yield opportunities change across chains, the system can automatically rebalance portfolios while generating proofs that demonstrate the rebalancing decisions were made according to user-defined parameters.

Implementation Results and Performance

Mainnet Deployment and User Adoption

NetworkNoya has successfully launched a live vault on mainnet, optimizing stablecoin curve pairs across multiple chains.[22] This deployment represents one of the first production implementations of zkML in DeFi yield optimization, providing real-world validation of the technology's viability.

Performance Metrics: The platform has demonstrated the ability to:

- Process complex multi-chain yield strategies in real-time
- Generate zkML proofs for strategy execution within acceptable

timeframes
- Maintain competitive yields while providing cryptographic verification
- Handle significant user deposits without performance degradation

Backtesting Verification: One of NetworkNoya's most innovative features is verifiable backtesting. Traditional DeFi platforms often present backtesting results that users must trust. NetworkNoya uses zkML to generate proofs of backtesting accuracy, providing auditable evidence of strategy performance.[23]

Trust and Security Outcomes

Reduced Trust Assumptions: The implementation has successfully demonstrated how zkML can eliminate the need for users to trust strategy managers with their funds. Users can verify that:

- AI models are executing according to specified parameters
- No unauthorized changes are made to strategy logic
- Risk management rules are properly enforced
- Fee structures are transparent and verifiable

Model Privacy Protection: The zkML implementation allows NetworkNoya to maintain the confidentiality of their proprietary AI models while still providing verification of correct execution. This protection of intellectual property creates a sustainable competitive advantage while maintaining user trust.[24]

Challenges and Solutions

Computational Complexity

Proof Generation Overhead: One of the primary challenges in NetworkNoya's implementation has been managing the computational overhead of generating zero-knowledge proofs for complex AI model execution. The team has addressed this through:

- Model optimization to reduce computational requirements

- Selective proof generation for critical decision points
- Off-chain computation with on-chain verification
- Hardware acceleration for proof generation

Real-Time Requirements: DeFi markets move rapidly, requiring quick decision-making capabilities. NetworkNoya has balanced this need through:

- Optimistic execution with slashing mechanisms for incorrect behavior
- Batched proof generation for non-critical operations
- Pre-computed proofs for common strategy scenarios

Market Integration Challenges

Protocol Compatibility: Integrating with multiple DeFi protocols across different chains has required extensive technical work to:

- Standardize interfaces across different protocol designs
- Handle varying transaction finality requirements
- Manage different tokenomics and reward structures
- Ensure compatibility with evolving protocol upgrades

Liquidity Management: Optimizing liquidity across multiple chains while maintaining efficiency has involved:

- Dynamic routing optimization
- Slippage minimization strategies
- Bridge cost optimization
- Emergency exit mechanisms

Economic Impact and User Benefits

Democratization of Sophisticated Strategies

NetworkNoya's implementation demonstrates how zkML can democratize access to sophisticated financial strategies that were previously available only to institutions or highly technical users. The platform enables regular users to:

- Access complex multi-chain yield strategies without technical expertise
- Benefit from institutional-grade risk management
- Maintain custody of their assets while accessing professional-level strategies
- Verify that their funds are being managed according to agreed parameters

Fee Transparency and Optimization

The zkML implementation provides unprecedented transparency in fee structures and optimization. Users can verify:

- Actual fees paid across different protocols and bridges
- Performance attribution across different strategy components
- Risk-adjusted returns compared to benchmarks
- Transaction efficiency and optimization effectiveness

Future Development and Ecosystem Impact

Technology Advancement

NetworkNoya's ongoing development includes:

Enhanced AI Models: Continued development of more sophisticated prediction models that can:

- Incorporate more data sources and market signals
- Adapt to changing market conditions dynamically
- Provide more granular risk management capabilities
- Handle edge cases and market stress scenarios

Improved zkML Efficiency: Ongoing optimization of the zero-knowledge proof system to:

- Reduce proof generation time and computational requirements
- Expand the complexity of models that can be verified

- Enable real-time verification for time-sensitive strategies
- Support larger-scale operations with improved efficiency

Industry Influence

NetworkNoya's success has influenced the broader DeFi ecosystem by:

Setting New Standards: The platform has established new expectations for transparency and verifiability in AI-powered DeFi applications, encouraging other projects to adopt similar approaches.

Advancing zkML Adoption: By demonstrating practical zkML implementation in a production environment, NetworkNoya has contributed to broader understanding and adoption of zkML technology across the DeFi ecosystem.

Infrastructure Development: The platform's requirements have driven improvements in supporting infrastructure, including better zkML development tools, more efficient proof generation systems, and enhanced cross-chain communication protocols.

The NetworkNoya case study illustrates how zkML can transform traditional trust models in DeFi, enabling sophisticated AI-driven strategies while maintaining the trustless principles that make decentralized finance compelling. The platform's success demonstrates that zkML is ready for production deployment in complex financial applications, though continued optimization and infrastructure development remain important for broader adoption.

7.3 Academic and Open-Source Projects: Advancing zkML Through Collaborative Research

The Foundation of Open Innovation

The development of practical zkML systems has been significantly accelerated by collaborative academic research and open-source development. Unlike proprietary implementations, these projects have created shared knowledge bases, standardized frameworks, and publicly available tools that have become the backbone of the zkML ecosystem. This section examines key academic initiatives and open-source projects that have shaped the current state of zkML technology.

EZKL: Democratizing zkML Development

Project Overview and Architecture

EZKL, developed by zkonduit, represents one of the most successful open-source frameworks for implementing zero-knowledge machine learning. The project has evolved from academic research into a production-ready library that enables developers to create zero-knowledge proofs for deep learning models without specialized cryptographic expertise.[25]

The EZKL framework provides an end-to-end pipeline that:

- Accepts models in the Open Neural Network Exchange (ONNX) format
- Converts neural network architectures into efficient zk-SNARK circuits
- Generates proofs for model execution using the Halo2 proving system
- Enables verification of these proofs both on-chain and off-chain[26]

Technical Innovations and Performance

Circuit Optimization: EZKL has pioneered several optimization techniques that make zkML practical for real-world applications:

- **Quantization Strategies**: The framework implements sophisticated quantization approaches that balance accuracy with proving efficiency. While some precision is lost in the conversion from floating-point to fixed-point arithmetic, EZKL's quantization maintains model utility for most practical applications.
- **Lookup Table Optimization**: For commonly used functions like ReLU activations, EZKL employs lookup tables that significantly

reduce circuit complexity and proving time.

- **Efficient Circuit Layouts**: The framework includes an optimizer that simulates various circuit configurations to identify layouts that minimize resource usage while maximizing performance.[27]

Benchmark Performance: EZKL has demonstrated impressive performance metrics across different model types:

- **MNIST Models**: Proof generation for 99% accuracy MNIST models in approximately 4 seconds on standard hardware
- **ImageNet Scale**: First framework to achieve practical zkML at ImageNet scale, with 92.4% accuracy models provable in under 45 minutes
- **Memory Efficiency**: Significant reductions in memory requirements, with some benchmarks showing 98% less memory usage compared to alternative frameworks[28]

Developer Ecosystem and Adoption

Community Building: EZKL has cultivated a vibrant developer community through:

- Comprehensive documentation and tutorials
- Interactive Jupyter notebooks for hands-on learning
- Active Telegram community with over 1,000 members
- Regular workshops and hackathon participation[29]

Integration Success Stories: The framework has been successfully integrated into various projects:

- **CryptoIdol**: A demonstration application that uses EZKL to create an AI judge for singing competitions, providing immutable and verifiable scoring
- **NFT Verification**: Integration with platforms for verifiable AI-generated content authentication

- **DeFi Applications**: Use in various yield optimization and risk assessment platforms[30]

Challenges and Solutions

Scaling Limitations: Despite significant optimizations, EZKL still faces challenges with very large models:

- **Proof Generation Time**: While impressive for the field, proof generation for large models still requires substantial computational resources
- **Memory Requirements**: Although optimized, memory usage for complex models can still be prohibitive for some applications
- **Accuracy Trade-offs**: Quantization necessary for efficient circuit representation can impact model accuracy[31]

Ongoing Development: The EZKL team continues to address these challenges through:

- Remote proving services that leverage specialized hardware
- Continued optimization of the underlying Halo2 implementation
- Research into more efficient quantization strategies
- Development of model-specific optimization techniques

Daniel Kang's zkml Framework: Academic Rigor Meets Practical Implementation

Research Origins and Open Source Release

The zkml framework, developed by Daniel Kang and collaborators at Stanford University, represents a significant academic contribution to the field that has been made available to the broader community. Released as open-source software in April 2023, the framework emerged from peer-reviewed research focusing on scaling zero-knowledge proofs to realistic machine learning models.[32]

Technical Contributions and Innovations

Scaling Breakthrough: The framework was the first to demonstrate zkML at ImageNet scale, representing a crucial milestone in making zero-knowledge machine learning practical for real-world computer vision applications. Key achievements include:

- **Model Complexity**: Support for realistic neural network architectures including ResNet variants and mobile-optimized models
- **Accuracy Preservation**: Demonstration of 92.4% accuracy on ImageNet classification while generating zero-knowledge proofs
- **Performance Optimization**: 6x reduction in proving cost and 500x improvement in verification times compared to initial research prototypes[33]

Architectural Innovations: The framework introduces several novel approaches to zkML implementation:

- **Circuit Compilation Optimization**: Advanced techniques for converting neural network operations into efficient arithmetic circuits
- **Memory Management**: Innovative approaches to managing the large memory requirements of zkML applications
- **Verification Efficiency**: Optimizations that enable fast verification of complex model executions[34]

Research Impact and Academic Validation

Peer Review and Publication: The underlying research has undergone rigorous peer review, with publications in top-tier computer systems conferences. This academic validation provides confidence in the theoretical foundations and practical implementation approaches.

Reproducible Research: All code and experimental configurations have been made publicly available, enabling independent replication and validation of results. This transparency has accelerated adoption and further research by other academic groups.

Collaboration Network: The project has fostered collaboration between academic institutions and industry partners, creating a bridge between theoretical research and practical implementation needs.

Applications and Use Cases

Trustless ML Auditing: The framework enables verification of machine learning model execution without requiring trust in the service provider. Applications include:

- **Algorithmic Accountability**: Verification that social media recommendation algorithms operate as claimed
- **Medical AI Validation**: Proof that diagnostic AI systems are functioning correctly without revealing patient data
- **Financial Model Verification**: Auditing of AI-driven trading and risk assessment systems[35]

Decentralized ML Services: The framework enables new models for machine learning as a service:

- **Verifiable API Endpoints**: ML service providers can offer cryptographic proof of correct model execution
- **Decentralized Model Marketplaces**: Platforms where model creators can prove capabilities without revealing model details
- **Privacy-Preserving Inference**: Applications that require ML capabilities while maintaining strict data privacy[36]

The Awesome-zkML Repository: Curating Community Knowledge

Community-Driven Resource Aggregation

The awesome-zkml repository, maintained by Worldcoin, serves as the central hub for zkML community resources, representing a collaborative effort to organize and disseminate knowledge across the rapidly evolving field.[37] This initiative demonstrates the importance of community-driven documentation and resource sharing in emerging technical fields.

Content Organization and Scope

Comprehensive Coverage: The repository organizes resources across multiple categories:

- **Libraries and Frameworks**: Detailed listings of available zkML implementation tools
- **Research Papers**: Curated collection of academic publications and preprints
- **Tutorial Materials**: Educational content for developers at different skill levels
- **Community Projects**: Showcase of innovative applications and experimental implementations[38]

Quality Curation: Unlike general-purpose lists, the awesome-zkml repository maintains high standards for included content:

- **Verification Requirements**: All included projects must demonstrate working implementations
- **Documentation Standards**: Listed resources must include adequate documentation for community use
- **Regular Maintenance**: Active curation ensures outdated or broken links are removed

Community Engagement and Growth

Bi-weekly Community Calls: The repository organizes regular community calls that bring together researchers, developers, and practitioners to discuss recent developments, share challenges, and coordinate collaborative efforts. These calls have become a crucial forum for knowledge exchange and community building.[39]

Educational Initiatives: The repository serves as a foundation for educational programs:

- **Workshop Materials**: Resources for university courses and professional development programs
- **Hackathon Resources**: Curated lists of tools and tutorials for zkML hackathon participants
- **Contributor Guidelines**: Clear documentation for community members who want to contribute resources[40]

Benchmarking and Comparative Analysis Projects

EZKL's Benchmarking Initiative

In 2024, the EZKL team conducted comprehensive benchmarking of different zkML frameworks, providing the community with objective performance comparisons.[41] This initiative addressed a critical gap in the field by establishing standardized metrics and testing methodologies.

Methodology and Scope: The benchmarking study compared EZKL against other popular frameworks including Orion and RISC Zero across multiple dimensions:

- **Setup Complexity**: Evaluation of developer experience and ease of use
- **Proving Time**: Performance measurements across different model types and sizes
- **Memory Usage**: Resource efficiency analysis under various workloads
- **Model Accuracy**: Assessment of precision loss due to quantization and circuit conversion[42]

Key Findings: The study revealed significant performance differences between frameworks:

- **Speed Advantages**: EZKL demonstrated average proving speeds 65.88x faster than RISC Zero and 2.92x faster than Orion

- **Memory Efficiency**: EZKL used 63.95% less memory than Orion and 98.13% less than RISC Zero
- **Accuracy Trade-offs**: Different frameworks showed varying capabilities in balancing accuracy with proving efficiency[43]

Impact on Framework Development

Performance Optimization: The benchmarking results have driven improvements across all measured frameworks:

- **Competitive Pressure**: Public performance comparisons have encouraged optimization efforts
- **Best Practice Sharing**: Successful optimization techniques have been shared across the community
- **Standardization Efforts**: The benchmarking methodology has become a reference for future evaluations

User Decision Support: The comparative analysis provides developers with objective criteria for framework selection based on their specific requirements and constraints.

Privacy-Scaling Explorations (PSE) Research Program

Ethereum Foundation Initiative

The Privacy and Scaling Explorations team at the Ethereum Foundation has launched several research initiatives focused on practical zkML applications. These projects represent significant investment in open research that benefits the entire ecosystem.[44]

Research Focus Areas: PSE's zkML research encompasses:

- **Scalability Solutions**: Research into more efficient proving systems for large-scale ML applications
- **Privacy-Preserving Applications**: Development of zkML systems that enhance user privacy in blockchain applications

- **Infrastructure Development**: Creation of tools and frameworks that lower barriers to zkML adoption[45]

Open Research Proposals

Real-World Model Porting: PSE has issued requests for proposals focusing on porting practical ML models into zero-knowledge systems. One notable example involves developing zkML systems for weather prediction using polarimetric radar data, addressing real-world infrastructure needs in developing countries.[46]

Methodology Development: These initiatives contribute to the development of standardized approaches for:

- **Model Selection**: Criteria for determining which ML models are suitable for zkML implementation
- **Performance Optimization**: Techniques for balancing accuracy, efficiency, and privacy in zkML systems
- **Integration Strategies**: Best practices for incorporating zkML into existing applications and infrastructure[47]

Lessons Learned from Academic and Open-Source Development

Technical Insights

Collaboration Accelerates Innovation: The open-source nature of academic zkML projects has accelerated development significantly compared to proprietary efforts. Shared code bases, open benchmarking, and collaborative problem-solving have led to faster optimization and broader adoption.

Standardization Importance: The success of frameworks like EZKL demonstrates the value of standardized interfaces and formats. The use of ONNX as a common model representation has enabled interoperability and reduced development friction.

Community-Driven Quality: Open-source projects with active communities have generally produced higher-quality, more reliable implementations than isolated development efforts.

Sustainability Challenges

Funding Models: Academic and open-source projects face ongoing challenges in securing sustainable funding for long-term development and maintenance. Successful projects have diversified funding through:

- Grant funding from foundations and government agencies
- Commercial partnerships and licensing arrangements
- Community donations and developer contributions[48]

Talent Retention: The competition for skilled zkML developers has created challenges for academic projects in retaining talent as commercial opportunities expand.

Future Directions

Infrastructure Development: Continued focus on developing shared infrastructure, including:

- Standardized testing frameworks for zkML implementations
- Common libraries for circuit optimization and proof generation
- Educational resources for new developers entering the field

Interdisciplinary Collaboration: Expanding collaboration between computer science, cryptography, and domain-specific researchers to address real-world application needs.

The academic and open-source contributions to zkML demonstrate the power of collaborative development in advancing complex technical fields. These projects have not only created practical tools but have also established the knowledge base and community structures necessary for continued innovation in zero-knowledge machine learning.

7.4 Emerging Use Cases: Polyhedra's EXPchain and the Future of Verifiable AI

The Evolution Toward AI-Native Blockchain Infrastructure

As zkML technology matures, a new generation of blockchain platforms is emerging that are purpose-built to support verifiable artificial intelligence applications. Polyhedra Network's EXPchain represents the most advanced example of this evolution, creating infrastructure specifically designed for scalable, verifiable, and privacy-preserving AI applications. This case study examines how dedicated AI blockchain platforms are addressing the limitations of retrofitting zkML onto existing infrastructure.

EXPchain: The "Everything Chain for AI"

Vision and Technical Foundation

EXPchain, launched on testnet in December 2024 with mainnet deployment scheduled for February 2025, represents a fundamental reimagining of blockchain infrastructure for the AI era.[49] Unlike existing platforms that attempt to add AI capabilities as an afterthought, EXPchain is designed from the ground up to support zero-knowledge machine learning as a native primitive.

The platform addresses three critical challenges in AI deployment:

- **Verifiability**: Ensuring AI systems are responsible and transparent through cryptographic proof
- **Privacy**: Protecting sensitive user data across AI applications while enabling verification
- **Performance**: Providing scalable infrastructure that can handle the computational demands of AI verification[50]

Revolutionary Technical Architecture

Expander Proof System: At the core of EXPchain's capabilities is the Expander proof system, which Polyhedra claims represents a breakthrough in zero-knowledge proof efficiency. The system demonstrates unprecedented performance metrics:

- 2.2 seconds per image for VGG-16 inference on a single-thread CPU
- 150 seconds per token for Llama-3.1 8B inference on a single-thread CPU
- Performance improvements of up to 4 orders of magnitude compared to previously reported results[51]

These performance improvements make previously impractical zkML applications viable for real-world deployment, representing a quantum leap in the practical applicability of verifiable AI.

zkPyTorch Integration: EXPchain introduces zkPyTorch, a compiler that seamlessly bridges traditional AI development with zero-knowledge proofs. This tool allows developers to:

- Import existing PyTorch models directly into zkML workflows
- Convert ONNX format models into zero-knowledge circuits automatically
- Maintain familiar development patterns while gaining zkML capabilities
- Reduce the specialized cryptographic knowledge required for zkML development[52]

Proof of Intelligence (PoI) Framework: EXPchain implements a novel consensus mechanism called Proof of Intelligence, which integrates machine learning directly into the blockchain's operation. This framework enables:

- Verification of AI model authenticity and integrity
- Tamper-proof certification of large language models processed through the chain
- Prevention of AI model fraud and unauthorized modifications
- Creation of an immutable chain of trust for AI systems[53]

Real-World Applications and Early Adopters

Gaming and Entertainment Applications

Zypher Network's Verifiable 2048: One of the first applications launched on EXPchain testnet is Zypher Network's implementation of a verifiable 2048 puzzle game. This application demonstrates how zkML can ensure fair play in gaming by providing cryptographic proof that game logic executes correctly without manipulation.[54]

The implementation showcases several key capabilities:

- Real-time proof generation for game state transitions
- Verification that random number generation is truly random and unbiased
- Prevention of cheating or game manipulation by any party
- Transparent reward distribution based on verifiable performance

AIdea Game Framework: AIdea Game is building the first comprehensive Verifiable AI Game Framework on EXPchain, focusing on fair play and transparent rewards powered by zkML technology. This framework addresses long-standing issues in gaming including:

- Verifiable artificial intelligence opponents that cannot be programmed to cheat
- Transparent algorithmic balancing that players can verify
- Immutable record of player achievements and progression
- Fair distribution of in-game assets and rewards[55]

Data Infrastructure and Cross-Chain Applications

KNN3Network Integration: KNN3Network is leveraging EXPchain to build secure blockchain ecosystems with a gateway to zkML-powered AI and zkBridge-enabled cross-chain data curation. Their implementation demonstrates how zkML can enhance data quality and verification across multiple blockchain networks.[56]

Key innovations include:

- Verifiable data aggregation across multiple blockchain networks
- AI-powered data quality assessment with cryptographic proof
- Privacy-preserving analytics on cross-chain data sets
- Transparent reputation systems for data providers

Dynamic Connectivity Solutions: Dynamic is developing seamless connectivity solutions for EXPchain that enable both blockchain natives and newcomers to interact with verifiable AI applications. Their approach addresses the user experience challenges that have limited zkML adoption.[57]

Financial and DeFi Applications

Cognitive Finance: Cognitive Finance is exploring AI-driven agents and intent-based actions for secure, streamlined financial management. Their EXPchain implementation focuses on:

- Verifiable execution of complex financial strategies
- Privacy-preserving analysis of user financial data
- Transparent risk assessment with AI models
- Automated compliance checking with regulatory requirements[58]

Lendvest Protocol: Lendvest is using deterministic zero-knowledge proofs to address transparency issues in DeFi transactions. Their implementation on EXPchain provides:

- Verifiable liquidation processes that protect user interests
- Transparent risk modeling for lending protocols
- Privacy-preserving credit assessment using zkML
- Auditable performance of algorithmic trading strategies[59]

Technical Achievements and Benchmarks

Performance Milestones

zkML Efficiency Records: EXPchain has achieved several performance records that establish new benchmarks for the industry:

- First platform to demonstrate practical zkML for billion-parameter language models
- Real-time proof generation for computer vision models
- Sub-second verification times for complex AI computations
- Practical deployment of zkML applications that were previously theoretical[60]

Scalability Demonstrations: The platform has demonstrated its ability to handle concurrent zkML applications without performance degradation:

- Multiple AI applications running simultaneously on testnet
- Consistent proof generation times under varying load conditions
- Efficient resource allocation across different AI workload types
- Scalable verification infrastructure supporting growing user bases

Innovation in AI Verification

Large Language Model Watermarking: EXPchain implements sophisticated watermarking techniques for large language models that enable:

- Verification of model authenticity without revealing model weights
- Detection of unauthorized model modifications or fine-tuning
- Proof of original model authorship and licensing compliance
- Prevention of model theft and unauthorized commercial use[61]

Cross-Chain AI Integration: The platform's zkBridge technology enables verifiable AI applications that span multiple blockchain networks:

- AI models that can access and verify data from multiple chains
- Cross-chain reputation systems for AI service providers
- Interoperable AI applications that maintain verification across networks
- Unified identity systems for AI agents operating across chains[62]

Industry Partnerships and Ecosystem Development

Strategic Collaborations

Ethereum Foundation Partnership: Polyhedra's collaboration with the Ethereum Foundation on the Expander Bootcamp demonstrates the alignment between EXPchain's technology and Ethereum's roadmap. The partnership focuses on:

- Application of Expander technology to Ethereum's planned BEAM chain
- Development of single-slot finality mechanisms using zero-knowledge proofs
- Post-quantum security research for blockchain applications
- Training programs for developers working on zkML applications[63]

Google Cloud Integration: The integration with Google Confidential Computing represents a significant advancement in combining traditional cloud infrastructure with zkML capabilities:

- Trusted Execution Environment (TEE) integration with zero-knowledge proofs
- Secure AI model execution in cloud environments with cryptographic verification
- Hybrid cloud-blockchain architectures for scalable zkML deployment
- Enterprise-grade security for sensitive AI applications[64]

Academic and Research Collaboration

Multi-Institutional Research: EXPchain development has involved collaboration with researchers from leading institutions including UC Berkeley, Stanford, Princeton, and Tsinghua University. This academic involvement ensures:

- Rigorous theoretical foundations for the platform's innovations
- Peer review and validation of technical claims
- Continuous research into next-generation zkML techniques

- Training of new researchers in zkML and verifiable AI[65]

Challenges and Future Development

Current Limitations

Hardware Requirements: Despite significant efficiency improvements, EXPchain applications still require substantial computational resources for proof generation:

- Specialized hardware remains beneficial for optimal performance
- Memory requirements for large model verification remain significant
- Energy consumption for proof generation needs continued optimization
- Cost barriers may limit adoption for smaller applications

Development Complexity: While zkPyTorch reduces barriers, developing zkML applications still requires:

- Understanding of zero-knowledge proof concepts
- Careful consideration of privacy and verification trade-offs
- Optimization expertise for efficient proof generation
- Integration complexity with existing AI development workflows

Roadmap and Future Capabilities

Enhanced Developer Tools: Planned improvements to the development experience include:

- Visual development environments for zkML application creation
- Automated optimization tools for circuit generation
- Integrated testing frameworks for zkML applications
- Simplified deployment pipelines for production systems[66]

Expanded AI Model Support: Future development will extend support to:

- Larger language models with improved efficiency

- Video and multimedia AI applications
- Real-time AI applications with instant verification
- Multi-modal AI systems combining different data types

Ecosystem Expansion: Plans for ecosystem growth include:

- Integration with traditional AI development frameworks
- Support for enterprise AI deployment requirements
- Standardized APIs for zkML service integration
- Marketplace platforms for verifiable AI services[67]

Implications for the Broader zkML Ecosystem

Infrastructure Precedent

EXPchain's approach establishes several important precedents for zkML infrastructure:

Native AI Support: The success of purpose-built AI blockchain infrastructure suggests that retrofitting existing platforms may not be optimal for zkML applications. Future blockchain platforms may increasingly incorporate AI verification as a core capability rather than an add-on feature.

Performance Standards: The performance achievements on EXPchain establish new expectations for zkML efficiency. These benchmarks will likely drive optimization efforts across the entire zkML ecosystem.

Developer Experience: The emphasis on developer-friendly tools demonstrates the importance of reducing barriers to zkML adoption. Successful zkML platforms must prioritize accessibility alongside technical capability.

Market Development

Enterprise Adoption: EXPchain's enterprise partnerships and regulatory-focused features suggest growing institutional interest in verifiable AI. This trend may accelerate as organizations seek to address AI transparency and accountability requirements.

Application Diversity: The range of applications being built on EXPchain demonstrates the broad applicability of zkML technology beyond its initial use cases in finance and identity verification.

Competitive Landscape: The success of dedicated AI blockchain platforms may encourage other projects to develop similar infrastructure, potentially leading to healthy competition and continued innovation.

Assessment and Future Outlook

Technical Validation

EXPchain's testnet deployment and early application success provide validation for several key hypotheses about zkML development:

Scalability Achievement: The platform demonstrates that zkML can scale to support multiple concurrent applications with acceptable performance characteristics.

Practical Applicability: Real-world applications running on the platform prove that zkML has moved beyond proof-of-concept to practical utility.

Developer Adoption: The growing ecosystem of applications suggests that development tools and infrastructure have reached sufficient maturity to support broader adoption.

Strategic Significance

Industry Leadership: Polyhedra's comprehensive approach to zkML infrastructure positions them as a leader in the emerging verifiable AI market. Their combination of research excellence, technical achievement, and ecosystem development creates significant competitive advantages.

Technological Advancement: The performance breakthroughs achieved with Expander suggest that continued optimization may soon make zkML practical for an even broader range of applications.

Market Validation: The successful deployment and growing adoption of EXPchain applications validate the market demand for verifiable AI infrastructure.

EXPchain represents a crucial milestone in the evolution of zkML from experimental technology to production-ready infrastructure. Its success demonstrates the viability of purpose-built AI blockchain platforms and establishes new standards for performance, developer experience, and application diversity. As the platform moves toward mainnet launch, its impact on the broader zkML ecosystem will likely be substantial, influencing both technical development and market adoption across the industry.

The case studies examined in this chapter demonstrate that zkML has evolved from academic research to practical, production-ready technology capable of addressing real-world challenges across diverse industries. From Worldcoin's global biometric verification system to NetworkNoya's sophisticated DeFi automation, from academic frameworks enabling widespread experimentation to purpose-built platforms like EXPchain, zkML is proving its value in creating more trustworthy, private, and verifiable AI systems. These implementations provide crucial insights into both the tremendous potential and current limitations of zkML technology, setting the stage for continued innovation and broader adoption across the AI and blockchain ecosystems.

Footnotes:

[1] World.org, "An introduction to zero-knowledge machine learning (ZKML)," World Blog, December 20, 2023, https://world.org/blog/engineering/intro-to-zkml.

[2] World.org, "Intro to zero-knowledge proofs, Semaphore and their application in World ID," World Blog, November 12, 2024, https://world.org/blog/world/intro-zero-knowledge-proofs-semaphore-application-world-id.

[3] World Whitepaper, "World ID is privacy preserving proof of human," accessed February 2025, https://whitepaper.world.org/.

[4] Ibid.

[5] BingX Blog, "What is Zero Knowledge Machine Learning (ZKML)?," July 31, 2023, https://blog.bingx.com/new-launch-analysis/what-is-zero-knowledge-machine-learning-zkml/.

[6] World Docs, "Zero-knowledge proofs," accessed February 2025, https://docs.worldcoin.org/further-reading/zero-knowledge-proofs.

[7] World.org, "Intro to zero-knowledge proofs, Semaphore and their application in World ID."

[8] European Parliament, "Parliamentary question | Worldcoin collecting biometric data," E-000961/2024, accessed February 2025, https://www.europarl.europa.eu/doceo/document/E-9-2024-000961_EN.html.

[9] Ibid.

[10] Biometric Update, "Iris biometrics crypto project Worldcoin reportedly looks for $120M investment," May 22, 2025, https://www.biometricupdate.com/202302/iris-biometrics-crypto-project-worldcoin-reportedly-looks-for-120m-investment.

[11] World Whitepaper, "World ID is privacy preserving proof of human."

[12] World.org, "Intro to zero-knowledge proofs, Semaphore and their application in World ID."

[13] World Whitepaper, "World ID is privacy preserving proof of human."

[14] ForkLog, "Worldcoin Aims for Global Biometric Verification Expansion," September 5, 2024, https://forklog.com/en/worldcoin-aims-for-global-biometric-verification-expansion/.

[15] ID Tech, "Tools for Humanity Acquires Modulus Labs to Boost Zero-Knowledge AI and Cryptography Research," December 12, 2024, https://idtechwire.com/tools-for-humanity-acquires-modulus-labs-to-boost-zero-knowledge-ai-and-cryptography-research/.

[16] Trader, "NOYA Network: AI-Powered Omnichain Yield Farming Revolution," accessed February 2025, https://vocal.media/trader/noya-network-ai-powered-omnichain-yield-farming-revolution.

[17] Ibid.

[18] NOYA Network, "Introduction to Zero-Knowledge Machine Learning," Medium, September 19, 2023, https://medium.com/@noyanetwork/introduction-to-zero-knowledge-machine-learning-177be20343ea.

[19] Homo_Sapien, "NOYA: Revolutionizing DeFi with AI-Powered Native Omnichain Yield Optimization," Medium, July 3, 2023, https://medium.com/@bmw21570/noya-revolutionizing-defi-with-ai-powered-native-omnichain-yield-optimization-29ced895aea.

[20] NOYA Network, "NOYA: Pioneering AI and ZKML-Driven Omnichain Yield Farming," Medium, June 26, 2023, https://medium.com/@noyanetwork/noya-pioneering-ai-and-zkml-driven-omnichain-yield-farming-ea2740d3b1fb.

[21] Ibid.

[22] Ibid.

[23] Homo_Sapien, "NOYA: Revolutionizing DeFi with AI-Powered Native Omnichain Yield Optimization."

[24] Ibid.

[25] GitHub, "zkonduit/ezkl: ezkl is an engine for doing inference for deep learning models and other computational graphs in a zk-snark (ZKML)," accessed February 2025, https://github.com/zkonduit/ezkl.

[26] Ibid.

[27] Zkrypto Inc., "ZKML: An Optimizing System for ML Inference in Zero-Knowledge Proofs," Medium, November 23, 2024, https://zkrypto.medium.com/zkml-an-optimizing-system-for-ml-inference-in-zero-knowledge-proofs-f9e4cafbefbe.

[28] Daniel Kang, "Open-sourcing zkml: Trustless Machine Learning for All," April 3, 2023, https://ddkang.github.io/blog/2023/04/03/open-source/.

[29] GitHub, "zkonduit/ezkl."

[30] Ibid.

[31] EZKL Blog, "Benchmarking ZKML Frameworks," accessed February 2025, https://blog.ezkl.xyz/post/benchmarks/.

[32] Daniel Kang, "Open-sourcing zkml: Trustless Machine Learning for All."

[33] Ibid.

[34] ACM Digital Library, "ZKML: An Optimizing System for ML Inference in Zero-Knowledge Proofs | Proceedings of the Nineteenth European Conference on Computer Systems," accessed February 2025, https://dl.acm.org/doi/10.1145/3627703.3650088.

[35] Daniel Kang, "Open-sourcing zkml: Trustless Machine Learning for All."

[36] Ibid.

[37] GitHub, "worldcoin/awesome-zkml: awesome-zkml repository," accessed February 2025, https://github.com/worldcoin/awesome-zkml.

[38] Ibid.

[39] Ibid.

[40] Ibid.

[41] EZKL Blog, "Benchmarking ZKML Frameworks."

[42] Ibid.

[43] Ibid.

[44] GitHub, "Proposal: Porting real-world ML model(s) into ZK · Issue #39 · privacy-scaling-explorations/acceleration-program," accessed February 2025,

https://github.com/privacy-scaling-explorations/acceleration-program/issues/39.

[45] Ibid.

[46] Ibid.

[47] Ibid.

[48] Daniel Kang, "Open-sourcing zkml: Trustless Machine Learning for All."

[49] Polyhedra Network, "Polyhedra: The Future of Intelligence," March 20, 2025, https://blog.polyhedra.network/the-future-of-intelligence/.

[50] Ibid.

[51] Polyhedra Network, "EXPchain Litepaper," accessed February 2025, https://docs.polyhedra.network/litepaper/.

[52] Messari, "State of Polyhedra Q4 2024," March 6, 2025, https://messari.io/report/state-of-polyhedra-q4-2024.

[53] Polyhedra Network, "EXPchain Litepaper."

[54] Polyhedra Network, "Building the future of intelligence: January 2025," February 4, 2025, https://blog.polyhedra.network/building-the-future-of-intelligence-january-2025/.

[55] Ibid.

[56] Ibid.

[57] Ibid.

[58] Ibid.

[59] Ibid.

[60] Polyhedra Network, "EXPchain Litepaper."

[61] Ibid.

[62] Polyhedra Network, "EXPchain," accessed February 2025, https://expchain.polyhedra.network/.

[63] Polyhedra Network, "Building the future of intelligence: January 2025."

[64] Polyhedra Network, "Trusted Execution Environment (TEE) in Polyhedra," May 14, 2025, https://blog.polyhedra.network/tee-in-polyhedra/.

[65] Polyhedra Network, "Polyhedra: The Future of Intelligence."

[66] Messari, "State of Polyhedra Q4 2024."

[67] Polyhedra Network, "Building the future of intelligence: January 2025."

Chapter 8: Future Directions and Research

The field of zero-knowledge machine learning stands at a pivotal juncture where cryptographic innovation meets artificial intelligence advancement. As we advance into 2025 and beyond, zkML is poised to undergo transformative developments that will fundamentally reshape how we approach privacy-preserving artificial intelligence. This chapter explores the emerging frontiers of zkML research, technological breakthroughs on the horizon, and the profound societal implications of these advancements.

The convergence of multiple technological trends—including quantum-resistant cryptography, specialized hardware acceleration, and the explosive growth of large language models—creates unprecedented opportunities for zkML evolution. Recent surveys indicate that the field has progressed from academic curiosity to practical implementation, with researchers achieving proof generation for models with up to 18 million parameters and the first successful verification of large language models on blockchain networks.[1]

8.1 Advancements in Efficiency

Hardware-Accelerated Proving Systems

The computational bottlenecks that have historically limited zkML adoption are rapidly dissolving through revolutionary hardware acceleration developments. The emergence of specialized zero-knowledge processing units represents a paradigm shift analogous to the GPU revolution in machine learning training. Companies like Cysic are developing dedicated ZK hardware that promises computing power equivalent to fifty NVIDIA RTX 4090 GPUs in a single device, specifically optimized for zero-knowledge proof generation.[2]

Modern zkML proving systems face two primary computational challenges: Multi-Scalar Multiplication (MSM) operations and Fast Fourier Transform (FFT) computations. MSM operations can consume over 60% of proving runtime, while FFT operations account for approximately 30%.[3] Hardware acceleration addresses these bottlenecks through several approaches:

Field-Programmable Gate Arrays (FPGAs) offer superior energy efficiency and lower latency compared to traditional CPU implementations. Early benchmarks demonstrate that FPGA-based solutions can achieve 10-1000x acceleration for zkML workloads while consuming significantly less power than GPU alternatives.[4] The programmable nature of FPGAs allows them to adapt to evolving proof systems and cryptographic algorithms, making them particularly valuable for the rapidly changing zkML landscape.

Graphics Processing Units (GPUs) have emerged as the current workhorse for zkML acceleration. The integration of libraries like ICICLE into frameworks such as EZKL has demonstrated remarkable performance improvements, with MSM operations achieving 50x speedups compared to CPU implementations.[5] Companies like Ingonyama have pioneered open-source GPU acceleration libraries that enable developers to leverage hardware acceleration with minimal code modifications.

Application-Specific Integrated Circuits (ASICs) represent the ultimate optimization for zkML workloads. While traditionally viewed as inflexible, the emergence of programmable ASIC designs addresses the need for adaptability in the evolving zkML ecosystem. These chips can potentially deliver the performance benefits of dedicated hardware while maintaining sufficient flexibility to support multiple proving systems and cryptographic parameters.[6]

The development of TensorPlonk exemplifies the transformative potential of specialized zkML hardware. This "GPU for ZKML" achieves up to 1,000x speedups for certain model classes, reducing the proving cost for Twitter's recommendation system from $88,704 to approximately $30 per verification cycle.[7] Such dramatic efficiency improvements make previously impractical applications economically viable and open new possibilities for real-world zkML deployment.

Optimized Circuit Architectures

Beyond hardware acceleration, fundamental advances in circuit design are dramatically improving zkML efficiency. Modern zkML frameworks are moving beyond generic proving systems toward specialized architectures optimized for machine learning workloads. The development of custom gadgets for common ML operations—such as dot products, non-linear activations, and matrix multiplications—enables more efficient proof generation while maintaining cryptographic security guarantees.

The introduction of lookup tables for non-linear operations represents a significant advancement in circuit optimization. Traditional approaches to handling activation functions like ReLU required expensive constraint systems that could dramatically increase proving costs. Modern lookup-based approaches reduce these costs by orders of magnitude while maintaining the same level of cryptographic security.[8]

Hierarchical proof composition is emerging as another crucial optimization technique. Rather than proving entire model executions in a single monolithic proof, hierarchical approaches break computations into smaller, manageable components that can be proven independently and then composed into a final verification certificate. This approach not only improves proving efficiency but also enables better parallelization and distributed proving architectures.

8.2 Integration with Emerging AI Trends

zkML for Large Language Models

The verification of large language models represents one of the most significant challenges and opportunities in zkML research. Recent breakthroughs have demonstrated the feasibility of generating zero-knowledge proofs for billion-parameter language models, with Modulus Labs achieving the first successful on-chain verification of a 1.5 billion parameter GPT2-XL model.[9] This milestone represents a crucial step toward practical zkLLM deployment.

The development of specialized proving systems for transformer architectures has been essential to these achievements. Traditional zkML approaches struggled with the attention mechanisms central to modern language models.

The introduction of zkAttn—a specialized zero-knowledge proof system designed specifically for attention computations—addresses these challenges by carefully balancing runtime, memory usage, and accuracy considerations.[10]

Future developments in zkLLM focus on several key areas:

Scalability to Modern Models: Current zkLLM implementations can handle models with up to 13 billion parameters, generating correctness proofs in under 15 minutes. However, state-of-the-art language models like GPT-4 and Claude contain hundreds of billions or potentially trillions of parameters. Scaling zkML to these model sizes requires fundamental advances in proof system efficiency and novel approaches to model decomposition.[11]

Streaming and Incremental Verification: Rather than proving entire model inferences in single proofs, future zkLLM systems may employ streaming verification approaches that generate proofs incrementally as tokens are generated. This approach could enable real-time verification of language model outputs while maintaining cryptographic guarantees.

Multi-Modal Extensions: As language models increasingly incorporate visual and audio processing capabilities, zkML systems must evolve to handle multi-modal computations. This expansion requires new proof techniques for image processing, audio analysis, and cross-modal reasoning while maintaining efficient verification.

Agentic AI and Self-Evolving Models

The emergence of agentic AI systems—autonomous agents capable of planning, reasoning, and executing complex tasks—presents new opportunities and challenges for zkML research. These systems often require verifiable decision-making processes, particularly when operating in high-stakes environments such as financial trading, healthcare diagnostics, or autonomous vehicle control.

zkML provides a natural framework for creating verifiable AI agents. By generating cryptographic proofs of their decision-making processes, AI agents can provide transparency and accountability while protecting proprietary algorithms and sensitive data. This capability is particularly valuable in regulatory environments that require auditable AI decision-making.

The development of self-evolving models—AI systems that can modify their own architectures and parameters based on new data and experiences—presents unique challenges for zkML systems. Traditional zkML approaches assume fixed model architectures that can be encoded into verification circuits. Self-evolving models require dynamic verification systems that can adapt to changing model structures while maintaining cryptographic security guarantees.

Research in this area focuses on several promising directions:

Functional Commitments for Dynamic Models: Rather than committing to specific model parameters, functional commitment schemes allow verification of model behavior without revealing architectural details. This approach enables verification of self-evolving models while preserving intellectual property and preventing model extraction attacks.[12]

Compositional Verification: Large agentic AI systems often consist of multiple specialized models working in concert. Compositional verification techniques enable these systems to generate proofs that individual components performed correctly while maintaining privacy about the overall system architecture.

Continuous Learning with Privacy: As AI systems learn and adapt continuously, zkML techniques must evolve to handle incremental updates while preserving privacy about training data and model evolution. This requires new approaches to proof aggregation and incremental verification.

8.3 Broader Ecosystem Development

Standards and Framework Development

The maturation of zkML as a practical technology requires the establishment of comprehensive standards and frameworks that ensure interoperability, security, and reliability across different implementations. Currently, the zkML ecosystem consists of numerous specialized frameworks—including EZKL, Circom, and proprietary solutions from companies like Modulus Labs—each with distinct approaches to proof generation and verification.

The development of standardized APIs and interfaces will be crucial for widespread zkML adoption. Just as machine learning frameworks like TensorFlow and PyTorch established common interfaces for model development and deployment, zkML requires similar standardization to enable seamless integration across different platforms and applications.

Several key areas require standardization:

Proof System Interoperability: Different zkML frameworks currently use incompatible proof systems, making it difficult to verify proofs generated by one system using another system's verifier. Standardized proof formats and verification protocols would enable cross-platform compatibility and reduce integration complexity.

Security Parameter Guidelines: The security of zkML systems depends on careful selection of cryptographic parameters, circuit designs, and trusted setup procedures. Standardized guidelines for these parameters would help developers avoid common security pitfalls and ensure consistent security levels across different implementations.

Performance Benchmarking: Comprehensive benchmarking standards are essential for comparing different zkML approaches and tracking performance improvements over time. Current benchmarking efforts focus primarily on proving time and memory usage, but future standards should include metrics for accuracy preservation, circuit complexity, and energy consumption.[13]

The development of open-source reference implementations will play a crucial role in establishing these standards. Projects like the awesome-zkml repository serve as community hubs for sharing research, code, and best practices, fostering collaboration and accelerating technological development.[14]

Quantum-Resistant zkML Designs

The eventual emergence of cryptographically relevant quantum computers poses a significant long-term challenge for zkML systems. Most current zero-knowledge proof systems rely on cryptographic assumptions that would be broken by sufficiently powerful quantum computers, including discrete logarithm problems and certain lattice-based constructions.

The transition to post-quantum cryptography is already underway in other areas of cybersecurity, with NIST having finalized the first three post-quantum encryption standards in August 2024.[15] These standards—based on lattice problems, hash functions, and other quantum-resistant mathematical foundations—provide a roadmap for developing quantum-resistant zkML systems.

Several promising approaches are emerging for post-quantum zkML:

Hash-Based Zero-Knowledge Proofs: Cryptographic hash functions are generally considered quantum-resistant when used with sufficiently large key sizes. Hash-based zero-knowledge proof systems like SPHINCS+ provide a foundation for building quantum-resistant zkML systems, though they typically require larger proof sizes and longer verification times compared to current approaches.[16]

Lattice-Based Constructions: Many post-quantum cryptographic schemes rely on lattice problems that are believed to be difficult for both classical and quantum computers. Recent research has explored adapting these constructions for zero-knowledge proofs, potentially providing a path toward quantum-resistant zkML systems.[17]

Hybrid Approaches: During the transition period, hybrid systems that combine classical and post-quantum cryptographic techniques may provide the best balance of security and performance. These systems could gradually migrate to fully post-quantum implementations as the technology matures and quantum computing threats become more imminent.

The timeline for quantum computer development remains uncertain, with expert predictions ranging from 10 to 30 years for cryptographically relevant systems.[18] However, the potential for "harvest now, decrypt later" attacks—where adversaries collect encrypted data today with the intention of decrypting it once quantum computers become available—creates urgency for developing post-quantum zkML solutions.

Ecosystem Governance and Regulatory Frameworks

As zkML transitions from research prototype to production deployment, the development of appropriate governance structures and regulatory frameworks becomes increasingly important. The unique properties of zkML—combining artificial intelligence with cryptographic privacy guarantees—create novel challenges for existing regulatory approaches.

Current regulatory frameworks for artificial intelligence often emphasize transparency and explainability, potentially conflicting with the privacy-preserving nature of zkML systems. Regulatory bodies must develop new approaches that balance the need for AI accountability with the legitimate privacy requirements that drive zkML adoption.[19]

Several regulatory trends are shaping the zkML landscape:

Privacy-First Regulation: Jurisdictions like the European Union are implementing comprehensive privacy regulations that may favor zkML approaches over traditional AI systems. The General Data Protection Regulation (GDPR) and similar frameworks create strong incentives for deploying privacy-preserving AI technologies.

AI Accountability Requirements: Emerging AI governance frameworks increasingly require organizations to demonstrate the reliability and safety of their AI systems. zkML provides a mechanism for proving AI system behavior without revealing proprietary algorithms or sensitive training data.

Cross-Border Data Transfer Restrictions: As governments implement stricter controls on cross-border data transfers, zkML enables international AI collaboration while keeping sensitive data within jurisdictional boundaries. This capability may become increasingly valuable as data sovereignty concerns continue to grow.

The development of industry self-regulation initiatives will also play a crucial role in zkML ecosystem governance. Organizations like the Post-Quantum Cryptography Alliance and emerging zkML industry groups are working to establish best practices, security standards, and ethical guidelines for zkML development and deployment.

8.4 Societal Impact and Trustworthy AI

Enabling Trustworthy AI in Regulated Sectors

The deployment of zkML in highly regulated sectors represents one of the most significant opportunities for societal impact. Healthcare, finance, and government applications often involve sensitive data and require high levels of accountability, making them natural candidates for zkML solutions.

Healthcare Applications: zkML enables the development of powerful diagnostic and treatment recommendation systems while preserving patient privacy. Hospitals and research institutions can collaborate on building robust models using aggregated patient data without violating privacy regulations or exposing individual medical records. Recent research has demonstrated zkML applications for medical imaging analysis, drug discovery, and epidemiological modeling while maintaining HIPAA compliance.[20]

Financial Services: The financial sector faces increasing pressure to demonstrate fairness and transparency in algorithmic decision-making while protecting customer privacy. zkML enables banks and financial institutions to prove that their lending, fraud detection, and risk assessment algorithms operate correctly without revealing proprietary methodologies or customer data. This capability is particularly valuable for regulatory compliance and building consumer trust.[21]

Government and Public Services: Government agencies can use zkML to provide transparent and accountable public services while protecting citizen privacy. Applications include welfare benefit determination, tax fraud detection, and public health monitoring. zkML enables these agencies to demonstrate that their AI systems operate fairly and without bias while maintaining appropriate privacy protections.

The success of zkML in these regulated sectors will largely depend on the development of appropriate certification and auditing frameworks. Regulatory bodies must establish processes for validating zkML systems and ensuring their continued reliability and security. This may require new forms of technical expertise and novel auditing approaches that can verify cryptographic proofs while assessing AI system performance.

Research Gaps and Future Challenges

Despite significant progress, several fundamental research challenges must be addressed to realize the full potential of zkML technology:

Scalability Limitations: Current zkML systems can handle models with millions to billions of parameters, but scaling to the largest contemporary AI systems remains challenging. The computational overhead of proof generation grows significantly with model size, and novel approaches to proof compression and aggregation are needed to make zkML practical for the largest AI systems.

Accuracy Preservation: Converting machine learning models to zero-knowledge circuits often introduces approximations and precision limitations that can impact model accuracy. Research is needed to minimize these accuracy losses while maintaining efficient proof generation. This challenge is particularly acute for applications requiring high precision, such as scientific computing and financial modeling.[22]

Economic Sustainability: The computational costs of zkML proof generation remain high compared to traditional AI inference. While hardware acceleration is reducing these costs, achieving economic viability for widespread deployment requires continued optimization. New economic models may be needed to distribute these costs fairly among stakeholders who benefit from zkML's privacy and verifiability guarantees.

Usability and Developer Experience: Current zkML frameworks require specialized knowledge of both machine learning and cryptography, limiting their accessibility to mainstream developers. Future research must focus on creating more user-friendly tools and abstractions that enable ML practitioners to deploy zkML solutions without deep cryptographic expertise.

Security and Formal Verification: As zkML systems handle increasingly sensitive applications, ensuring their security becomes critical. This requires formal verification of zkML implementations, comprehensive security audits, and the development of standardized security testing procedures. The complexity of zkML systems—combining AI and cryptographic components—creates novel attack surfaces that must be carefully analyzed and protected.

Long-Term Vision and Societal Transformation

The long-term impact of zkML extends far beyond technical improvements to AI systems. As the technology matures, it has the potential to fundamentally transform how society approaches data privacy, AI transparency, and digital trust.

Democratization of AI Development: zkML could enable smaller organizations and developing nations to participate in AI development without compromising sensitive data. By allowing secure collaboration on AI projects while preserving data sovereignty, zkML may help distribute the benefits of AI more equitably across the global community.

New Economic Models: The ability to prove AI system behavior without revealing proprietary algorithms creates opportunities for new forms of intellectual property protection and revenue sharing. AI developers could potentially license their models' capabilities without revealing implementation details, enabling new forms of collaboration and competition.

Enhanced Digital Rights: zkML supports the development of AI systems that respect individual privacy rights while providing valuable services. As digital rights frameworks evolve, zkML may become an essential technology for implementing privacy-preserving AI that complies with emerging regulations and ethical standards.

Scientific Collaboration: The scientific community could benefit enormously from zkML-enabled collaboration on sensitive datasets. Researchers could jointly develop models using confidential data from multiple institutions while preserving privacy and intellectual property rights. This capability could accelerate scientific discovery in fields like epidemiology, climate science, and social research.

The realization of these transformative impacts will require continued collaboration among researchers, industry practitioners, policymakers, and civil society organizations. The technical challenges of zkML development must be coupled with careful consideration of ethical implications, regulatory requirements, and societal needs.

As we advance into the next decade, zkML stands poised to play a central role in shaping the future of artificial intelligence. The convergence of improving hardware, maturing cryptographic techniques, and growing demand for privacy-preserving AI creates an unprecedented opportunity to build AI systems that are simultaneously powerful, private, and trustworthy. The research directions outlined in this chapter represent crucial steps toward realizing this vision and ensuring that the benefits of advanced AI can be enjoyed while preserving fundamental values of privacy, accountability, and human dignity.

The path forward requires sustained investment in fundamental research, the development of practical tools and standards, and thoughtful consideration of the societal implications of this transformative technology. As zkML continues to evolve, it promises to reshape not only how we build AI systems but how we think about the relationship between technological capability and human values in an increasingly digital world.

Footnotes:

[1] Wang Taotao et al., "A Survey of Zero-Knowledge Proof Based Verifiable Machine Learning," arXiv preprint arXiv:2502.18535 (2025), https://arxiv.org/abs/2502.18535.

[2] "ZK DePIN Hardware Acceleration and Compute Power Network Leader Cysic," Gate.io Learn, May 20, 2024, https://www.gate.io/learn/articles/zk-depin-hardware-acceleration-and-compute-power-network-leader-cysic/2937.

[3] "Hardware Review: GPUs, FPGAs and Zero Knowledge Proofs," Ingonyama, accessed September 2025, https://www.ingonyama.com/post/hardware-review-gpus-fpgas-and-zero-knowledge-proofs.

[4] "Hardware Acceleration for Zero Knowledge Proofs," Paradigm, April 13, 2022, https://www.paradigm.xyz/2022/04/zk-hardware.

[5] "Steps in Hardware, Leaps in Performance," EZKL Blog, accessed September 2025, https://blog.ezkl.xyz/post/acceleration/.

[6] Omer Shlomovits, "Revisiting Paradigm 'Hardware Acceleration for Zero Knowledge Proofs'," Medium, September 19, 2023, https://medium.com/@omershlomovits/revisiting-paradigm-hardware-acceleration-for-zero-knowledge-proofs-16f717a49555.

[7] Daniel Kang, "TensorPlonk: A 'GPU' for ZKML, Delivering 1,000x Speedups," Medium, September 21, 2023, https://medium.com/@danieldkang/tensorplonk-a-gpu-for-zkml-delivering-1-000x-speedups-d1ab0ad27e1c.

[8] "ZKML: An Optimizing System for ML Inference in Zero-Knowledge Proofs," Zkrypto Inc., Medium, November 23, 2024, https://zkrypto.medium.com/zkml-an-optimizing-system-for-ml-inference-in-zero-knowledge-proofs-f9e4cafbefbe.

[9] "Chapter 14: The World's 1st On-Chain LLM," Modulus Labs, Medium, March 14, 2024, https://medium.com/@ModulusLabs/chapter-14-the-worlds-1st-on-chain-llm-7e389189f85e.

[10] Haochen Sun, Jason Li, and Hongyang Zhang, "zkLLM: Zero Knowledge Proofs for Large Language Models," arXiv preprint arXiv:2404.16109 (2024), https://arxiv.org/abs/2404.16109.

[11] Ibid.

[12] "ZKML Research Initiatives," HackMD, accessed September 2025, https://hackmd.io/@cathie/zkml-research.

[13] "A Survey of Zero-Knowledge Proof Based Verifiable Machine Learning," arXiv preprint arXiv:2502.18535 (2025).

[14] "An introduction to zero-knowledge machine learning (ZKML)," Worldcoin Blog, December 20, 2023, https://world.org/blog/engineering/intro-to-zkml.

[15] "NIST Releases First 3 Finalized Post-Quantum Encryption Standards," NIST, August 13, 2024, https://www.nist.gov/news-events/news/2024/08/nist-releases-first-3-finalized-post-quantum-encryption-standards.

[16] "Post-quantum cryptography in Red Hat Enterprise Linux 10," Red Hat, May 20, 2025, https://www.redhat.com/en/blog/post-quantum-cryptography-red-hat-enterprise-linux-10.

[17] "Post-Quantum Zero-Knowledge and Signatures from Symmetric-Key Primitives," ResearchGate, October 30, 2017, https://www.researchgate.net/publication/320679475_Post-Quantum_Zero-Knowledge_and_Signatures_from_Symmetric-Key

[18] "Post-Quantum Cryptography (PQC): New Algorithms for a New Era," Rambus, April 14, 2025, https://www.rambus.com/blogs/post-quantum-cryptography-pqc-new-algorithms-for-a-new-era/.

[19] "What is AI Governance?" IBM, July 29, 2025, https://www.ibm.com/think/topics/ai-governance.

[20] "ZKML: Verifiable Machine Learning using Zero-Knowledge Proof," Kudelski Security, April 8, 2025, https://kudelskisecurity.com/modern-ciso-blog/zkml-verifiable-machine-learning-using-zero-knowledge-proof/.

[21] "Decentralized Zero-Knowledge Machine Learning: Implications and Opportunities," Struck Capital, January 21, 2025, https://struckcapital.com/decentralized-zero-knowledge-machine-learning-implications-and-opportunities/.

[22] "Zero-Knowledge Machine Learning (ZKML) - HeLa," HeLa Labs, October 20, 2023, https://helalabs.com/blog/zero-knowledge-machine-learning-zkml/.

Appendices and Resources

Appendix A: Comprehensive Glossary

This glossary provides definitions for key terms in zero-knowledge machine learning (zkML), drawing from established cryptographic and AI concepts. Definitions are based on verifiable sources from academic papers, industry documentation, and technical specifications to ensure accuracy.

Arithmetic Circuit: A representation of a computation as a set of gates (e.g., addition, multiplication) over finite fields, used in ZKPs to model programs for proof generation. Often employed in zk-SNARKs for efficient verification.

Backpropagation: An algorithm used in training neural networks to compute gradients and update model weights by propagating errors backward through the network layers.

Bulletproofs: A type of zero-knowledge proof system that enables range proofs and other computations without a trusted setup, known for short proofs and efficiency in certain applications.

Circom: A domain-specific language and compiler for writing arithmetic circuits compatible with zk-SNARKs, commonly used in zkML frameworks to convert ML models into provable circuits.

Completeness: A property of ZKPs ensuring that if the statement is true and both parties follow the protocol, the verifier will accept the proof with high probability.

Computational Integrity: The assurance that a computation (e.g., ML inference) was performed correctly, verifiable without re-executing the full process, central to zkML applications.

Convolutional Neural Network (CNN): A type of deep learning model specialized for processing grid-like data, such as images, using convolutional layers to extract features.

Decision Tree: A machine learning model that makes predictions by recursively splitting data based on feature values, often used in zkML for privacy-preserving predictions.

Deep Learning: A subset of machine learning involving neural networks with multiple layers, capable of learning complex patterns from large datasets.

EZKL: A library and command-line tool for doing inference for deep learning models and other computational graphs in a zk-SNARK, enabling end-to-end zkML workflows.

Federated Learning: A distributed ML approach where models are trained across multiple devices or servers without sharing raw data, enhanced by zkML for verifiable aggregation.

Fiat-Shamir Heuristic: A technique to convert interactive proofs into non-interactive ones by using hash functions to simulate the verifier's challenges.

Halo2: A proving system based on PLONK, used in zkML frameworks for generating proofs of ML executions, supporting custom gates for efficiency.

Inference: The process of applying a trained ML model to new data to generate predictions or outputs, often the focus of zkML proofs to verify results privately.

Large Language Model (LLM): Advanced neural networks trained on vast text data for tasks like generation and comprehension, with zkML enabling verifiable outputs.

Lookup Tables: Pre-computed tables used in zkML to handle non-linear operations efficiently within zero-knowledge circuits, trading memory for computational efficiency.

Model Inversion Attack: A privacy threat where adversaries reconstruct training data from a model's outputs, mitigated by zkML's privacy guarantees.

Neural Network: A computational model inspired by biological neurons, consisting of interconnected layers that process inputs to produce outputs.

ONNX (Open Neural Network Exchange): An open format for representing ML models, used in zkML to convert models from frameworks like PyTorch into ZKP-compatible forms.

PLONK: A universal zk-SNARK system with a trusted setup, allowing for efficient proofs across various computations, including ML models.

Polynomial Commitment: A cryptographic primitive where a party commits to a polynomial and can later prove evaluations without revealing the full polynomial.

Prover: In a ZKP, the party that generates the proof to convince the verifier of a statement's truth without revealing underlying data.

Quantization: The process of converting floating-point model parameters to fixed-point representations suitable for zero-knowledge circuits, often involving precision trade-offs.

R1CS (Rank-1 Constraint System): A system for representing computations as quadratic equations over finite fields, foundational for many zk-SNARK implementations in zkML.

Soundness: A ZKP property ensuring that if the statement is false, no malicious prover can convince an honest verifier, except with negligible probability.

Succinctness: A characteristic of ZKPs where proofs are short and verification is fast, crucial for zkML scalability on blockchains.

TensorPlonk: An optimization framework for zkML that delivers significant speedups through specialized handling of matrix operations and non-linearities.

Training: The phase in ML where a model learns parameters from data, less common in zkML due to computational intensity but explored in verifiable training setups.

Trusted Setup: A ceremony in certain ZKP systems where public parameters are generated, requiring trust that the setup was performed correctly.

Verifier: In a ZKP, the party that checks the proof's validity without learning private information.

Zero-Knowledge Machine Learning (zkML): The integration of ZKPs with ML to prove computations (e.g., inference) were performed correctly while keeping inputs, models, or outputs private.

Zero-Knowledge Proof (ZKP): A cryptographic method allowing a prover to demonstrate knowledge of a value or statement's truth to a verifier without conveying additional information.

zk-SNARK (Zero-Knowledge Succinct Non-Interactive Argument of Knowledge): A ZKP variant that is succinct, non-interactive, and requires a trusted setup, widely used in zkML for efficient proofs.

zk-STARK (Zero-Knowledge Scalable Transparent Argument of Knowledge): A ZKP system that is transparent (no trusted setup) and post-quantum secure, suitable for large-scale zkML computations.

zkPyTorch: A hierarchical optimized compiler for zero-knowledge machine learning that seamlessly integrates ML frameworks like PyTorch with ZKP engines.

Appendix B: Tools, Frameworks, and Libraries

This appendix provides a comprehensive overview of tools and frameworks available for zkML development, organized by category and functionality.

Core zkML Frameworks

EZKL

- **Description**: A library and CLI tool for zk-SNARK inference on deep learning models
- **GitHub**: https://github.com/zkonduit/ezkl
- **Features**: ONNX model support, Halo2 backend, production-ready Lilith cluster
- **Performance**: MNIST models in ~6 seconds, 1.1GB RAM usage
- **Status**: Production-ready with 200k+ daily proofs

zkPyTorch (2025)

- **Description**: Hierarchical optimized compiler integrating PyTorch with ZKP engines
- **Research**: ePrint IACR 2025/535
- **Performance**: VGG-16 in 2.2 seconds per CIFAR-10 image, Llama-3 150s per token
- **Innovation**: Automated ML-to-ZKP conversion with optimization

zkml (Daniel Kang)

- **Description**: Framework for constructing proofs of ML model execution
- **GitHub**: https://github.com/ddkang/zkml
- **Performance**: MNIST circuit in ~16 seconds, 5GB memory
- **Research**: Based on "Scaling up Trustless DNN Inference" paper

Circuit Development Tools

Circom

- **Description**: Domain-specific language for zk-SNARK circuit development
- **Website**: https://circom.io/
- **Use Case**: Converting ML operations into arithmetic circuits
- **Ecosystem**: Extensive library support for ML operations

circomlib-ml

- **Description**: Library for ML circuits in Circom
- **GitHub**: https://github.com/socathie/circomlib-ml
- **Features**: Neural network layer templates, activation functions
- **Maintainer**: Privacy & Scaling Explorations (PSE)

keras2circom

- **Description**: Tool to transpile TensorFlow Keras models into Circom circuits
- **GitHub**: https://github.com/socathie/keras2circom
- **Integration**: Direct Keras to zkML conversion pipeline

Proving Systems and Backends

Halo2

- **Description**: PLONK-based proving system with lookup arguments
- **Advantages**: Efficient handling of non-linearities, no trusted setup for new circuits
- **Usage**: Primary backend for EZKL and many zkML frameworks

RISC Zero

- **Description**: General-purpose zkVM targeting RISC-V instruction set
- **GitHub**: https://github.com/risc0/risc0
- **zkML**: SmartCore ML integration for Rust-based models
- **Advantage**: General-purpose computation support

Plonky2

- **Description**: Fast recursive SNARK implementation
- **Performance**: Optimized for large-scale proving workloads

- **Usage**: High-performance applications requiring fast proof generation

Specialized zkML Projects

Orion (Giza Tech)

- **Description**: Cairo-based ZKML framework
- **GitHub**: https://github.com/gizatechxyz/orion
- **Features**: STARK-based proofs, Cairo VM integration
- **Advantage**: Transparent (no trusted setup)

Bionetta (Rarimo)

- **Description**: R1CS-based proving framework for client-side zkML
- **Focus**: Neural network verification with on-chain checks
- **Performance**: Benchmarked for practical applications

Zator

- **Description**: System for verified inference on 512-layer neural networks
- **GitHub**: https://github.com/lyronctk/zator
- **Innovation**: Recursive SNARKs for deep networks

Development and Testing Tools

zkml-framework-benchmarks

- **Description**: Comprehensive benchmarking suite for zkML frameworks
- **GitHub**: https://github.com/zkonduit/zkml-framework-benchmarks
- **Features**: Standardized performance comparisons across frameworks

brain-bench-runner

- **Description**: Python benchmarking tool for popular zkML frameworks
- **GitHub**: https://github.com/inference-labs-inc/brain-bench-runner
- **Features**: Automated benchmarking with GitHub Actions integration

Libraries and Supporting Tools

Libsnark

- **Description**: C++ library for zk-SNARK constructions
- **Use Case**: Low-level ZKP development for ML applications

Winterfell

- **Description**: STARK prover/verifier library
- **Integration**: Used with Giza's tooling for Cairo-based zkML

Bulletproofs

- **Description**: Range proof system without trusted setup
- **Application**: Specific zkML use cases requiring range constraints

Appendix C: Real-World Projects and Case Studies

Production Deployments

Worldcoin World ID

- **Technology**: zk-SNARKs for biometric verification
- **Innovation**: Proving human uniqueness without storing biometric data
- **Scale**: Global deployment with millions of verifications
- **Framework**: Custom iris recognition with zero-knowledge proofs

NetworkNoya (DeFi)

- **Application**: AI-powered yield optimization with verifiable strategies
- **Technology**: zkML for transparent algorithmic trading
- **Impact**: Trustless DeFi protocols with AI intelligence

EXPchain (Polyhedra)

- **Platform**: zkML testnet for verifiable AI applications
- **Features**: Hardware acceleration, privacy-preserving identity
- **Status**: Active testnet with growing developer ecosystem

Research and Development Projects

PSE ZKML

- **Organization**: Privacy & Scaling Explorations (Ethereum Foundation)
- **Focus**: Fundamental zkML research and tool development
- **Contributions**: circomlib-ml, theoretical foundations

Inference Labs

- **Specialization**: Healthcare AI verification ensuring HIPAA compliance
- **Innovation**: Model complexity reduction for medical imaging
- **Impact**: Enabling private healthcare AI deployment

Axiom

- **Technology**: Trustless access to on-chain data with ZKPs
- **Integration**: Supporting zkML applications in Web3 ecosystem

Academic and Open Source Initiatives

ZKaggle/ZKaggleV2

- **Description**: Decentralized bounty platform for ML tasks with

privacy
- **GitHub**: https://github.com/z-kaggle/ZKaggle, https://github.com/socathie/ZKaggleV2
- **Innovation**: Kaggle-like platform preserving data privacy

zk-mnist

- **Description**: Educational zkML implementation for MNIST dataset
- **GitHub**: https://github.com/0xZKML/zk-mnist
- **Purpose**: Learning and demonstration of zkML concepts

proto-neural-zkp

- **Organization**: Worldcoin
- **Description**: zkML experiments with Plonky2
- **GitHub**: https://github.com/worldcoin/proto-neural-zkp
- **Focus**: Advanced neural network proving techniques

Appendix D: Performance Benchmarks and Metrics

Framework Comparison (2024-2025 Data)

Framework	Model Type	Proving Time	Memory Usage	Accuracy Preservation
EZKL	MNIST	6 seconds	1.1GB	>99%
EZKL	VGG-16	Variable	Variable	>95%
zkPyTorch	VGG-16	2.2s/image	TBD	>98%
zkPyTorch	Llama-3	150s/token	TBD	>95%
zkml (Kang)	MNIST	16 seconds	5GB	>99%
RISC Zero	SmartCore Models	Variable	Variable	>95%

Scalability Metrics

EZKL Production (Lilith Cluster)

- Peak throughput: 200,000+ proofs per day
- Job dispatch time: <1ms across 200+ workers
- Uptime: 99.99% over 6+ months
- Geographic distribution: Multi-region deployment

Cost Analysis (2025)

- Traditional verification: ~\$88,704 for 6,000 Twitter model inferences
- TensorPlonk optimization: ~\$30 for same workload (1,000x improvement)
- Practical viability threshold: Achieved for many applications

Hardware Requirements

Minimum Requirements

- RAM: 8GB (for small models like MNIST)
- CPU: 4-core modern processor
- Storage: 10GB for frameworks and circuits

Recommended Production

- RAM: 64GB+ for large models
- CPU: 16+ cores with high clock speeds
- Storage: SSD with 100GB+ available space
- Network: High-bandwidth for distributed proving

Appendix E: Recent Research Papers and Publications

Foundational Surveys (2024-2025)

1. **"A Survey of Zero-Knowledge Proof Based Verifiable Machine Learning"**
    - arXiv:2502.18535 (2025)

   - Comprehensive overview of zkML landscape
2. **"Zero-Knowledge Proof Frameworks: A Survey"**
   - arXiv:2502.07063 (2025)
   - Comparative analysis of ZKP systems for ML
3. **"Zero-Knowledge Proof-based Verifiable Decentralized Machine Learning in Communication Network"**
   - arXiv:2310.14848 (2025 update)
   - Focus on decentralized applications

Technical Implementations

1. **"zkPyTorch: A Hierarchical Optimized Compiler for Zero-Knowledge Machine Learning"**
   - ePrint IACR 2025/535
   - Polyhedra Network's breakthrough compiler
2. **"An Optimizing System for ML Inference in Zero-Knowledge Proofs"**
   - ACM Proceedings (2024)
   - ZKML framework optimization techniques
3. **"Scalable Zero-knowledge Proofs for Non-linear Functions in Machine Learning"**
   - ePrint IACR 2025/507
   - Advanced techniques for complex ML operations

Application-Specific Research

1. **"Zero-knowledge machine learning models for blockchain peer-to-peer energy trading"**
   - Internet of Things and the Environment (2025)
   - Energy sector applications
2. **"Model Complexity Reduction for ZKML Healthcare Applications"**
   - Blockchain in Healthcare Today (2024)
   - Healthcare-specific optimizations

Performance and Benchmarking

1. **"Benchmarking ZKML Frameworks"**
   - EZKL Blog (2024)
   - Empirical comparison of major frameworks
2. **"TensorPlonk: A 'GPU' for ZKML, Delivering 1,000x Speedups"**
   - Medium/Research Publication (2023-2024)
   - Revolutionary performance improvements

Appendix F: Community Resources and Learning Materials

Educational Platforms

Awesome Lists

- **awesome-zkml**: https://github.com/worldcoin/awesome-zkml
- **awesome-zk**: https://github.com/ventali/awesome-zk
- **awesome-zkvm**: https://github.com/rkdud007/awesome-zkvm

Documentation and Tutorials

- EZKL Documentation: https://docs.ezkl.xyz/
- Circom Documentation: https://docs.circom.io/
- Zero-Knowledge University: Educational resources across platforms

Community Engagement

Discussion Forums

- ZKML Community Telegram: Active community discussions
- Research Discord servers: Academic and technical discussions
- GitHub Discussions: Framework-specific technical support

Conferences and Events

- ZK research conferences (annual)
- ZKML community calls (monthly)
- Academic workshops on privacy-preserving ML

Professional Development

Certification and Training

- Online courses in cryptography and ZKP
- ML privacy specializations
- Hands-on workshops with zkML frameworks

Research Opportunities

- Academic collaborations
- Open-source contributions
- Industry research partnerships

Appendix G: Regulatory and Compliance Framework

Data Protection Regulations

GDPR Compliance

- Article 25: Data protection by design and by default
- Article 32: Security of processing
- zkML applications for lawful basis demonstration

HIPAA Requirements

- Administrative safeguards alignment
- Technical safeguards through zkML
- Audit trail capabilities

Industry-Specific Regulations

- Financial services: SOX, Basel III implications
- Healthcare: FDA software validation
- Government: FISMA compliance considerations

Standards and Certifications

Emerging Standards

- ISO/IEC development for ZK systems
- NIST guidance on privacy-preserving computation
- Industry consortium standards

This comprehensive appendix provides practitioners, researchers, and students with the resources needed to engage with the rapidly evolving field of zero-knowledge machine learning. As the field continues to advance, these resources serve as a foundation for continued learning and development.

Bibliography

• "A Survey of Zero-Knowledge Proof Based Verifiable Machine Learning." arXiv preprint arXiv:2502.18535 (2025). https://arxiv.org/abs/2502.18535

• "A Survey on the Applications of Zero-Knowledge Proofs." ResearchGate publication (2024). https://www.researchgate.net/publication/382797463_A_Survey_on_the_Applications_of_Zero-Knowledge_Proofs

• "A Survey on Zero Knowledge Proofs and their applications on Machine Learning." Politecnico di Milano Thesis (2023). https://quattrocchi.faculty.polimi.it/papers/zk-survey.pdf

• "An introduction to zero-knowledge machine learning (ZKML)." Worldcoin Blog (2023). https://world.org/blog/engineering/intro-to-zkml

• "An Optimizing System for ML Inference in Zero-Knowledge Proofs." ACM Proceedings (2024). https://dl.acm.org/doi/10.1145/3627703.3650088

• "On-chain zero-knowledge machine learning: An overview and analysis." Journal of King Saud University - Computer and Information Sciences (2024). https://www.sciencedirect.com/science/article/pii/S1319157824002969

• "Open-sourcing zkml: Trustless Machine Learning for All." Daniel Kang Blog (2023). https://ddkang.github.io/blog/2023/04/03/open-source/

• "Research on Zero knowledge with machine learning." Journal of Computing and Engineering: Informatics and Management (2024). https://drpress.org/ojs/index.php/jceim/article/view/19445

• "Scalable Zero-knowledge Proofs for Non-linear Functions in Machine Learning." ePrint IACR (2025). https://eprint.iacr.org/2025/507.pdf

• "Zero Knowledge Machine Learning (zkML) Explained: What is zkML?" DroomDroom (2024). https://droomdroom.com/zero-knowledge-machine-learning-zkml-explained/

• "Zero Knowledge Proofs in Machine Learning: A Comprehensive Guide." SotaZK Insights (2024). https://sotazk.org/insights/zero-knowledge-proofs-in-machine-learning-a-comprehensive-guide/

• "Zero-Knowledge Machine Learning (ZKML): Projects Exploring the Space." Medium Article (2023). https://bwetzel.medium.com/zero-knowledge-machine-learning-zkml-projects-exploring-the-space-fc9d5f04fb65

• "Zero-Knowledge Machine Learning (ZKML) is Revolutionizing Privacy in Finance." Medium Article (2024). https://xthemadgenius.medium.com/zero-knowledge-machine-learning-zkml-is-revolutionizing-privacy-in-finance-b443c1175f76

• "Zero-Knowledge Machine Learning: Bridging Privacy and Verification in AI Systems." Medium Article (2025). https://medium.com/@aannkkiittaa/zero-knowledge-machine-learning-bridging-privacy-and-verification-in-ai-systems-e8cb8bc5f610

• "Zero-knowledge machine learning models for blockchain peer-to-peer energy trading." Internet of Things and the Environment (2025). https://www.sciencedirect.com/science/article/pii/S2542660525001520

• "Zero-Knowledge Proof-Based Verifiable Decentralized Machine Learning." Semantic Scholar (2024).

https://www.semanticscholar.org/paper/add1f31cdb20cc3c228fcec490b2367484bb95ac

• "ZKML: Verifiable Machine Learning using Zero-Knowledge Proof." Kudelski Security Blog (2025). https://kudelskisecurity.com/modern-ciso-blog/zkml-verifiable-machine-learning-using-zero-knowledge-proof/

• "zkPyTorch: A Hierarchical Optimized Compiler for Zero-Knowledge Machine Learning." ePrint IACR (2025). https://eprint.iacr.org/2025/535

• "zkTaylor: Zero Knowledge Proofs for Machine Learning via Taylor Polynomial Approximation." ACM Proceedings (2025). https://dl.acm.org/doi/10.1145/3712623.3712646

Don't miss out!

Did you love *Zero-Knowledge Machine Learning (zkML): Revolutionizing Privacy in AI Applications*? Then you should read *Learn AI Fast: A Practical Guide for Busy Professionals*[1] by Dr Naim Tahir Baig!

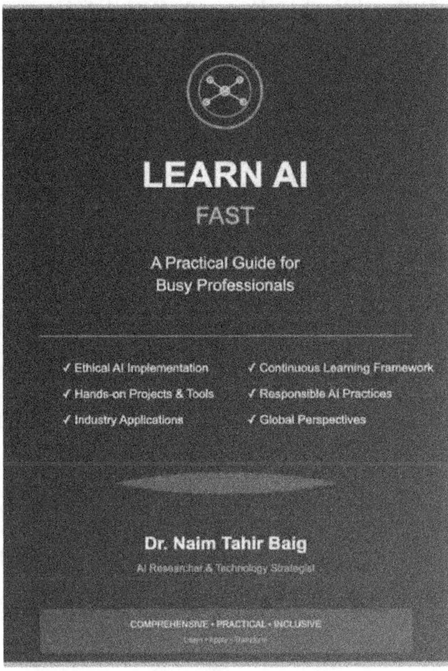

[2]

LEARN AI FAST: A Practical Guide for Busy Professionals

Book Description

In an era where artificial intelligence is reshaping every industry, professionals across all sectors face a critical choice: adapt and thrive, or risk being left behind. "Learn AI Fast" provides the comprehensive yet accessible roadmap that busy professionals need to navigate this technological transformation successfully.

Dr. Naim Tahir Baig, a renowned Author, AI researcher and strategist, has distilled years of experience implement AI solutions into a practical, step-by-step guide that respects your time constraints while delivering real expertise. Unlike technical manuals that overwhelm or superficial overviews

1. https://books2read.com/u/bxXKGd
2. https://books2read.com/u/bxXKGd

that underwhelm, this book strikes the perfect balance—providing deep understanding without unnecessary complexity.

What Makes This Book Different:

This isn't just another AI book written by technologists for technologists. Dr. Baig understands that real AI literacy means more than knowing how to use tools—it means understanding how to apply AI ethically, effectively, and inclusively in diverse professional contexts.

The RAPID Framework: At the heart of the book is the evidence-based RAPID methodology (Recognize, Apply, Practice, Iterate, Deploy), which has been tested and refined across thousands of professionals globally. This framework transforms AI learning from overwhelming complexity into manageable, progressive skill development that fits into busy professional lives.

Comprehensive Coverage: From understanding AI fundamentals and mastering prompt engineering to implementing responsible AI practices and advancing your career, this book covers everything professionals need to become confident AI practitioners. Real case studies from organizations like Commonwealth Bank, Petrobras, and Microsoft demonstrate how systematic AI adoption creates measurable business value while maintaining ethical standards.

Inclusive and Global Perspective: Written with awareness that AI's impact spans cultures, industries, and experience levels, this book addresses bias mitigation, accessibility considerations, and diverse implementation approaches. Whether you're in São Paulo or Stockholm, Mumbai or Minneapolis, the frameworks adapt to your context while maintaining universal applicability.

Immediate Practical Value: Every chapter includes hands-on exercises, implementation checklists, and actionable strategies you can apply immediately. From the marketing coordinator who needs to streamline content creation to the operations manager implementing predictive maintenance, readers gain skills that translate directly into professional impact.

Future-Focused Learning: Beyond current tools and techniques, Dr. Baig prepares readers for continuous adaptation in a rapidly evolving field. The book's emphasis on developing meta-skills, building learning communities, and maintaining ethical foundations ensures that your AI competency remains relevant regardless of technological changes.

Read more at https://www.naimtahirbaig.com.

Also by Dr Naim Tahir Baig

1

Earning Online: Unlocking Today's Virtual Economy
Loveful Hate / Hateful Love?
A Textbook Of Foreign Policy Analysis

Standalone

Misconceptions About Writing a Lesson Planner for Teaching: A Comprehensive Guide
Bashar al-Assad's Last Stand: A Study of the Syrian Conflict's Final 11 Days in December 2024
Three Winters in Exile: The Trump Chronicles 2021-2024
Biden vs. Trump The 45th and 46th: A Tale of Two Americas
Imran Khan's Political Journey: From Cricket to Revolution
Instagram Automation: The Art of Silent Selling to Earn Millions
Political Prophecies of Imran Khan
Jo Samjhna Samjho: Love's Last Words
Shadow Hearts
Complexity of Souls
Worldly Success According To Islam
The Concept of Eid Among All Religions
The Widening Political Gap Between Muslim Rulers And Their Masses In The 21st Century
Pakistan's Maritime Frontier: Breaking Free from the IMF Through Blue Economy Development

Can Russia Help Pakistan Grow?
Why Nuclear-Armed Pakistan Has Not Fought a War Against Israel in the 2020s?
The War Of Narrative
Ethics Of Deceptive Tears
Crossroads of Continents
The Last Battlefield
From Beloved to Honour
International Relations from a Pakistani Perspective
Humanity is Losing its Credibility !
Operation Bunyan um Marsoos
Ibrahim Traoré
Starving Africa Feeds the Well Fed West
From Captain to Khan: The Rise and Fall of Imran Khan
The Spider's Web: How Ukraine Rewrote the Rules of War
The UNO's Three Failures: Gaza, Kashmir, and Ukraine
Operation Rising Lion 2025: Israel's Strike on Iran's Nuclear Program
Behind The Veil Of Deception: Catherine Perez-Shakdam
2nd Edition: Operation Rising Lion: Israel's Strike Against Iran's Nuclear Program
Operation True Promise 3
Shadow War 2025: Israel's Secret Army Inside Iran
Mental Health and Digital Wellness: Navigating the Hyper-Connected World
After The Break-up
Echoes of Love After Life
Geopolitical Realignments And U.S. Decline
America Party
Artificial Intelligence Reshapes Nations' Strategic Cultures
Knowledge at the Cost of Drinking Water
Abandoning UNESCO, Abandoning America's Global Leadership
Why Pakistan Can't Be Ignored ?
Love Seized
Tarifaço: Trump's Tariff Assault on Brazil and the Battle for Hemispheric Power
GAZA: The word 'ETHICS' is at stake

Kiss Cam Crisis
The Boomer Blockade: How an Aging Generation is Reshaping Global Power and Economics at Younger Generations' Expense
Fractured Faith: The Ken Paxton Divorce Scandal and the Crisis of Conservative Authenticity
The New American Empire In 2025
The Last Rock's Secret War: Okinotorishima and Japan's Fight for Tomorrow's Ocean
The Great Realignment
Trump's Siege on the Fed: Politics, Power, and the Fracturing of Global Finance
Nuclear Weapons in Space
Trump vs. Putin: The Secrets Of Alaska Summit 2025
Nuclear Orbits: From Soviet Satellites to Russian Space Power
Learn AI Fast: A Practical Guide for Busy Professionals
Rare Earth Metals in Pakistan: Geopolitics in the New Great Game
The Kulbhushan Affair: Espionage, Diplomacy, and Justice in the Shadow of South Asian Rivalry
Collision Over the Capital: The Untold Story of the 2025 Potomac River Mid-Air Disaster and the Fight for Safer Skies
The Holy Qur'an, Political Fire: The Extremism of Valentina Gomez
World War I of Climate Change: Geopolitical Parallels and Emerging Battles
International Relations: Theoretical Frameworks in the Pakistani Context
Equal and Orderly Multipolarization of the World: The Shanghai Cooperation Organization as a Catalyst
Selbstgehostete E-Mail-Server: Praxisanleitung für Datenschutz und Unabhängigkeit in Deutschland
From Gaza's Siege to Pakistan's Floods 2025: An Islamic Perspective on Collective Accountability and Calamities
Hero's Wings Over the 1965 War: Air Commodore Haider's Story
Zero-Knowledge Machine Learning (zkML): Revolutionizing Privacy in AI Applications

Watch for more at https://www.naimtahirbaig.com.

About the Author

Dr. Naim Tahir Baig can be described as a Political Analyst, Geopolitical Strategist, Military and Security Studies Expert, Intelligence and Espionage Scholar, Social Commentator, Philosopher of Contemporary Issues, Digital Economy Specialist, Islamic Scholar and Interfaith Commentator, Poet and Literary Author, Regional Studies Expert, Multidisciplinary Intellectual, and Pakistan-Centric Analyst, reflecting his diverse expertise across politics, geopolitics, military strategy, intelligence, social commentary, business, religion, literature, and regional studies.

Published Books of Dr. Naim Tahir Baig

Learn AI Fast: A Practical Guide for Busy ProfessionalsNuclear Orbits: From Soviet Satellites to Russian Space PowerTrump vs. Putin: The Secrets Of Alaska Summit 2025Nuclear Weapons in SpaceTrump's Siege on the Fed: Politics, Power, and the Fracturing of Global FinanceThe Great RealignmentThe Last Rock's Secret War: OkinotorishimaThe New American Empire In 2025Fractured Faith: The Ken Paxton Divorce Scandal and the Crisis of Conservative AuthenticityThe Boomer Blockade: How an Aging Generation is Reshaping Global Power and Economics at Younger Generations' ExpenseKiss Cam CrisisGAZA: The word 'ETHICS' is at stakeTarifaço: Trump's Tariff Assault on Brazil and the Battle for Hemispheric PowerLove SeizedWhy Pakistan Can't Be Ignored ?Abandoning UNESCO, Abandoning America's Global LeadershipKnowledge at the Cost of Drinking WaterArtificial Intelligence Reshapes Nations' Strategic CulturesAmerica PartyGeopolitical Realignments And U.S. DeclineEchoes of Love After LifeAfter The Break-upMental Health and Digital Wellness: Navigating the Hyper-Connected WorldShadow War 2025: Israel's Secret Army Inside IranOperation True Promise 32nd Edition: Operation Rising Lion: Israel's Strike Against Iran's Nuclear ProgramBehind The Veil Of Deception: Catherine Perez-ShakdamOperation Rising Lion 2025: Israel's Strike on Iran's Nuclear Program

Read more at https://www.naimtahirbaig.com.

www.ingramcontent.com/pod-product-compliance
Lightning Source LLC
LaVergne TN
LVHW022035200926
848481LV00003B/700
* 9 7 9 8 2 3 2 6 4 7 8 5 8 *